PRAISE FOR
The Unlikely Art of Parental Pressure

"*The Unlikely Art of Parental Pressure* is the rare parenting book that respects both parents and children. Instead of simply applauding parental pressure as the key to success or dismissing it as cruel and ineffective, Thurber and Weisinger walk their readers through the theory and practice of parenting happy, successful children. A tour de force."

—ABBY FREIREICH and BRIAN PLATZER,
education columnists for *The Atlantic* and the
authors of *Taking the Stress out of Homework*

"*The Unlikely Art of Parental Pressure* beautifully illuminates and addresses the delicate dance that parents are faced with on a daily basis."

—Chad Beguelin, playwright and lyricist of *The Prom*

"Parental pressure is often detrimental to a child's desire to participate in sports. This book provides parents the tools to transform parental pressure into a positive force that will encourage your child to follow their passion and perform their best, be it on the soccer field or school field."

—GREGG BERNHALTER, head coach,
U.S. Men's National Soccer Team

"All parents worry that they are pushing their children too much . . . or not enough. Two sophisticated psychologists, Drs. Thurber and Weisinger, tackle this problem head-on in *The Unlikely Art of Parental Pressure*. With up-to-date science, great wisdom, and readable case examples, they show parents the right way to support their children. If you have ever worried that you are the dreaded 'pushy parent,' you should read this book. Your children will thank you."

—MICHAEL G. THOMPSON, PHD, bestselling
author of *Raising Cain* and *Best Friends; Worst Enemies*

"There is an 'art' to parental pressure, and Drs. Thurber and Weisinger give you the brushstrokes and tools you need to become a master at healthy prodding that supports children and avoids harmful results or pushback. One of the most helpful parenting books of the last decade."

—SUSAN NEWMAN, PHD, social psychologist and
author of *Little Things Long Remembered:
Making Your Children Feel Special Every Day*

"This is a great resource for any parent who wants to know how to push their kids to do their best without placing their children under toxic pressure."

—AMY MORIN, author of *13 Things Mentally Strong
Parents Don't Do* and *13 Things Strong Kids Do*

"Based on their decades of experience, Drs. Thurber and Weisinger have illuminated a new pathway to student success by demystifying the difference between healthy and harmful parental pressure. *The Unlikely Art of Parental Pressure* invites readers to a conversation about parenting that can improve the lives of parents and children as they both strive to be their best."

—TYLER CHAPMAN TINGLEY, EdD,
thirteenth principal of Phillips Exeter Academy,
first co-head, Avenues: The World School

"How do we push children without pressuring them in unhealthy ways? How might we support without being too lenient? Amid the onslaught of unsolicited, unscientific, and often conflicting advice, parents feel confused in answering these questions. Enter the warm and humorous advice of Drs. Thurber and Weisinger. By the end of the book, you'll have absorbed the parental trifecta: compassion, clarity, and scientifically backed guidance to transform unhealthy pressure into wise parenting."

—YAEL SCHONBRUN, PhD, assistant professor,
Brown University, and cohost of the
Psychologists Off the Clock podcast

"Drs. Thurber and Weisinger's work teaches parents how to transform unhealthy parental pressure into a guiding force that will help any child navigate their life more effectively and, in the process, boost the quality of the parent-child relationship."

—GILDA ROSS, student and community projects
coordinator, GlenBard Parent Series

"No one goes to school to be a parent, hence the African saying that 'it takes a village to raise a child.' This book is timely during this pandemic, when many children are casualties of Covid-19. Reading the book reminded me that children are essential for the survival of our species—a sober reminder for those in schools where the focus is raising children in partnership with parents and guardians."

—TEMBA MAQUBELA, headmaster at Groton School

"*The Unlikely Art of Parental Pressure* is a timely, insightful exploration of a challenge that all parents face as they help navigate their children's journey toward success. The book provides a broad and deep examination of issues that parents will immediately resonate with and offers practical solutions that parents can actually use with themselves and their children."

—JIM TAYLOR, PhD, author of *Positive Pushing:
How to Raise a Successful and Happy Child*

"With a keen eye to the never-easy dynamics of parenting kids with potential, Thurber and Weisinger show a better way to avoid the paradox of harming our kids when all we really want is to make their lives easier than our own."

— MICHAEL UNGAR, PHD, director, Resilience Research Centre, Dalhousie University; author, *Change Your World: The Science of Resilience and the True Path to Success*

"Like the ghost of Christmases Past, Present, and Future, Thurber and Weisinger guide you behind the scenes to give you a panoramic view of the effects parental pressure can have on our children. While reading this book, you may also uncover the residual footprints of your own parents' parenting style. Thurber and Weisinger enlighten and educate, teaching us how to reframe and convey our positive intentions in a way that fosters a healthy and supportive space for our children to thrive."

— BRITTNEY-NICHOLE CONNOR-SAVARDA, founder, Catalyst 4 Change; Generation EQ

The Unlikely Art of
Parental Pressure

A Positive Approach
to Pushing Your Child
to Be Their Best Self

CHRIS THURBER, PhD
AND
HENDRIE WEISINGER, PhD

hachette
BOOKS

New York

Hachette Go, an imprint of Hachette Books
Hachette Book Group
1290 Avenue of the Americas
New York, NY 10104
HachetteGo.com
Facebook.com/HachetteGo
Instagram.com/HachetteGo

First Edition: July 2021

Hachette Books is a division of Hachette Book Group, Inc.

The Hachette Go and Hachette Books name and logos are trademarks of Hachette Book Group, Inc.

The publisher is not responsible for websites (or their content) that are not owned by the publisher.

Print book interior design by Linda Mark

Library of Congress Cataloging-in-Publication Data
Names: Thurber, Christopher A., 1968– author. | Weisinger, Hendrie, author.
Title: The unlikely art of parental pressure : a positive approach to pushing your child
  to be their best self / Christopher Thurber, PhD, and Hendrie Weisinger, PhD.
Description: First edition. | New York, NY : Hachette Go, [2021] | Includes
  bibliographical references and index.
Identifiers: LCCN 2021003076 | ISBN 9780306874772 (paperback) |
  ISBN 9780306874789 (ebook)
Subjects: LCSH: Parenting. | Social pressure. | Expectation (Psychology) | Self-esteem
  in children. | Success in children.
Classification: LCC HQ755.8 .T5658 2021 | DDC 649/.1—dc23
LC record available at https://lccn.loc.gov/2021003076

ISBNs: 978-0-306-87477-2 (trade paperback); 978-0-306-87478-9 (ebook)

Printed in the United States of America

LSC-C

Printing 1, 2021

*For Simonida, the best co-parent and friend anyone could hope for.
And for Dacha and Sava, whose praise and criticism have energized
and inspired me; whose forgiveness and humor have given me faith;
and whose manner of treating others makes me eternally proud.*

*To Bri and Danny, who have enriched my life immeasurably,
and to Josh, Alex, Sammy, Sherry, Robbie, Ian, Molly, Peri, Talia,
Catey, and Meredith, who have done the same for their parents.*

CONTENTS

AUTHORS' NOTES

Our Story and Style
(. . . and a bunch of terms we need to define)

YOU MIGHT IMAGINE THAT TWO PSYCHOLOGISTS WRITING A BOOK about parental pressure are engaged in some kind of public catharsis. But neither of us endured a traumatic childhood. You might also imagine that we are delusional, believing we did such a flawless job with our own children that we can graciously bestow our successes on the world. Hardly. Like every parent, we have made our share of mistakes, including in the pressure department. Therefore (and thankfully), this book is neither group therapy nor humblebrag. Instead, *The Unlikely Art of Parental Pressure* is a normalization of our species' instinct to want the best for its offspring, as well as a recognition that caregiving instincts can derail healthy parenting. And because parenting derailments can hurt children and prevent them from becoming their best selves, this book is decidedly practical. Even the title is more functional than flowery. The *unlikely* part refers to the conventional wisdom that all pressure is harmful pressure and that harmful pressure is intentional. As unlikely as it may seem, neither of these popular notions is true. The *art* part refers to parents' necessity to improvise and customize. Human relationships are complicated, ever-changing puzzles where each person's behavior influences the other person's behavior. To keep it fairly healthy and happy, we must adjust, usually on the fly.

This book might be the first to begin with the author(s) simultaneously asserting that parental instincts can backfire *and* confessing that parents make stuff up as they go along. That sounds scarily akin to telling a driver that the gas pedal sometimes acts like a brake, but to relax anyway because there is not much of a visible road to begin with. Luckily, *The Unlikely Art of Parental Pressure* is not a freewheeling rant. Instead, we have written fourteen concise chapters in a logical sequence, gradually introducing the eight parenting transformations most strongly linked to excellent performance and great mental health. Our introduction and epilogue bracket the chapters within a sociocultural framework. In addition, we have grounded this book in research, despite our appreciation for the complexities of young humans and despite our recognition that every parent-child relationship has mysteries that science has yet to explain. Finally, we have written from our hearts, endeavoring on every page to speak authentically, parent to parent.

To contextualize our perspectives, we have included brief biographies next. Knowing that other parents' diverse backgrounds shape alternate perspectives, we encourage all readers to share their parental pressure experiences and differing points of view on DrChrisThurber.com/Pressure.

DR. CHRISTOPHER THURBER
Harvard, '91; UCLA, '97

I grew up on the Maine coast. The older of two boys, I attended South Portland public schools from kindergarten through twelfth grade. My classmates were ethnically homogenous (mostly white, with a few first-generation immigrants) and largely working-class and middle-class. Most of my courses were above average in quality and moderately competitive, with rigorous sciences and parochial humanities. I feel blessed that my family was able to travel, both within and outside the US, to provide experiences for my brother and me that deepened our understanding of people, geography, politics, language, prejudice, and world cultures.

My parents—a psychiatric nurse and a family doctor—were entrepreneurs, both having started their own clinical practices after working in hospitals. They set high academic and character standards for me through their examples, so the pressure I felt was a constant, implicit expectation to follow suit. Whatever athletic and artistic activities I chose, my parents were supportive, frequently attending games, meets, and performances. Usually, their emphasis was on my effort more than the outcome, but I did love overhearing them tell my grandparents about my accomplishments in swimming and piano.

When my parents separated in high school, I coped with the uncertainty by putting tremendous pressure on myself to perform well academically. In 1986, I started college at Wesleyan University. At that time, many students there cared more about partying and virtue signaling than about academics, and enough were silently competitive to create an unpleasant stoner/cutthroat vibe. Many students felt peer pressure to become someone they were not. I spent the following year in Normandy, France, living with two generous host families and attending the Université de Caen Normandie. After earning a diploma in French, I transferred to Harvard University to complete a bachelor's degree in psychology. I experienced the pressure at Harvard as healthy, robust, and driven by the unspoken narrative, "This school has top-tier teachers and facilities, so any shortcomings in your performance are entirely your own."

Following graduation, I returned to work my sixth summer at Camp Belknap, then spent nine months as a research assistant for a professor who was studying autism at UMass Boston. In 1992, I moved across the country to attend UCLA for graduate school. I completed my PhD internship in clinical psychology at Children's Hospital and Regional Medical Center (now Seattle Children's) and enjoyed a two-year postdoctoral fellowship in rehabilitation psychology at the University of Washington School of Medicine. Shortly after, I began expanding my summer leadership position at Belknap to include educational work with camps and schools all over the world. In 1999, I accepted a position as a psychologist and instructor at Phillips Exeter Academy, an independent school in seacoast New Hampshire. I estimate that I have taught Introduction to Psychology more than thirty times and provided psychotherapy to nearly 2,500 different students, many of whom have described intense pressure. But it was my research on another universal malady—homesickness—that first captured attention. My homesickness-prevention programs—now hosted on Prep4Camp.com and Prep4School.com—landed me guest appearances on CNN, *Today*, NPR, *Martha*, Fox 25, *CBS This Morning*, *Canada AM* (Toronto), and *The Bund* (Shanghai).

My wife and best friend, Simonida, who had emigrated from Serbia a few years before we met, is a chemist, a musician, and a lovingly dedicated mother. Together, we have two boys, Dacha (b. 2002) and Sava (b. 2004), who attended Exeter public schools and then Phillips Exeter Academy for grades nine through twelve. Our parenting styles complement each other, with Simonida offering the boys more detailed guidance and encouraging the kind of sustained effort that builds virtuosity; and my offering the boys more opportunities for exploration and the kind of healthy risk-taking that boosts self-confidence. Like my coauthor, Hank, Simo and I do our best to parent lovingly, learn from our mistakes, and understand how our kids experience our parenting.

DR. HENDRIE WEISINGER

Windham College, '70; Alfred University, '72; University of Kansas, '78

I grew up in Great Neck, Long Island. I graduated from Great Neck North High School, which I experienced as highly competitive. My parents rarely monitored my homework, but they used to say, "You're the only one who knows whether you're doing your best." Thus, the parental pressure I felt was indirect and tinged with a bit of guilt. Nevertheless, I cared more about playing and watching baseball and football than about academics. In fact, on the day of the PSATs, I went to an Army–Notre Dame game at Yankee Stadium with my father. On the way to the game, we passed my high school, and he saw some students and parents gathered outside. He asked me what was going on, and I replied, "I don't know." In retrospect, it seems my parents' brand of pressure was to let the natural consequences teach me important life lessons. Predictably, my grades suffered, and I was required to attend summer school to make up failed classes. Meanwhile, my friends worked hard and got into top colleges and universities. I graduated 409th out of 449 seniors.

In contrast to school, home was where my intellect and creativity thrived, partly because my parents asked open-ended questions and listened attentively to my answers. My father, the editor of DC's *Superman*, would bring me comics each evening, which I would read and reread voraciously. In the morning, over breakfast, he would test out new plot ideas with me. With great fondness, I remember "What if Superman did this?" discussions as an engaging and energizing way to start the day. My father and I also watched TV together, with him often asking me, "What motivated that character to make that decision?" or "How would you improve the story?" or "What's gonna happen next?" or "Can you guess the ending?" Years later, I found myself playing the same educational game with my own children, eventually turning the activity into an article for *TV Guide* called "Tutored by Television."

After high school, I attended Belknap College, where the students were either academic weaklings, chronic underachievers, or students that other colleges had kicked out. I was in the middle category. Needless to say, the pressure from my parents, my professors, and my peers was minimal—until I took a psychology class with an inspiring teacher. Then everything changed. For the first time in my life, being a student felt rewarding instead of onerous. I remember my mother saying to me, back in high school, "Someday, when you're truly interested in something, you'll feel motivated." As her internalized voice awoke inside my head and ignited some healthy pressure, I realized how prescient she was.

I later transferred to the more rigorous Windham College, earned a master's degree in school psychology from Alfred University, and completed a PhD from the University of Kansas. Since the mid-1990s, I have delighted in writing books and speaking about the practical applications of emotional intelligence. My parents would be proud to know that two of my books—*Performing Under Pressure: The Science of Doing Your Best When It Matters Most* and *Nobody's Perfect: How to Give Criticism and Get Results*—became *New York Times* best sellers.

I enjoy sharing my surprising discoveries about pressure, performance, and mental health because I see the benefit to individuals and institutions. Indeed, I have consulted and conducted workshops for dozens of Fortune 500 companies, government agencies, and professional organizations, such as YPO. I have also taught in business school executive education programs and executive MBA programs at Wharton, UCLA, Cornell, NYU, Penn State, and Columbia. My media appearances have included *Oprah, Today, Good Morning America*, ESPN, and NPR. I also enjoy teaching parents, couples, and corporate executives about giving feedback and managing anger. Like Chris, I love being a father. I have always tried to parent my own children with the same encouragement, freedom, and unconditional love that my parents gave me.

WRITING CONVENTIONS

We endeavored to write *The Unlikely Art of Parental Pressure* with a respectful tone, from an inclusive perspective, and peppered with humor. (Parenting without humor is like eating saltines without something to drink—it quickly goes from delicious to dry to dreadful.) Where representative research supports our assertions, we have provided endnotes. A few tangents were fascinating enough to deserve endnotes as well. Where precise definitions of unusual terms mattered, we have provided them in the text. To promote clarity and prevent misunderstandings, we have filled the next few pages with our definitions of common terms, our style conventions, and our construction of case examples.

Parent

Throughout the book, we use the word *parent* to refer to a child's primary caregiver(s), be they biologically related or not. Whereas *caregiver* can refer to any person—sibling, teacher, coach, clergy, mentor, relative, or family friend—who contributes to a child's development, the word *parent* carries the added cross-cultural meaning of "one who brings forth offspring" and "one who carries the primary responsibility for the upbringing of a child." Our use of *parent* makes no genetic, political, racial, ethnic, religious, gender, sexual, or legal assumptions. Although harmful pressure can be applied by different people (e.g., parent, peer, coach, teacher) and by culturally colored environmental elements (e.g., media, faith, language, workplace), we have chosen to focus on parents in this book because of their impressive contribution to children's development.

Pronouns

When we write from a shared perspective, we use the first-person plural pronoun, *we*. When I (Chris) present case examples, the pronoun switches to *I*. (Read more about case examples below.) Finally, whenever we refer to parents or children, we use the third-person plural, gender-inclusive pronouns *they*, *them*, and *theirs*, instead of a combination of gendered or novel third-person singular pronouns.

Anxiety and Worry

We use the term *anxiety* to mean a combination of uncomfortably tense emotions, agonizing thoughts about what will happen next, and unpleasant physiological arousal, such as trembling, racing heartbeat, sweating, and dizziness. Many people who experience anxiety try to avoid the source of their distress, although that is not always possible. Clinicians often make the distinction between *anxiety*, which is rather diffuse and primarily somatic (body-based), and *worry*, which is rather specific and primarily cognitive (thought-based). Thus, a student might be worried about how they will do on their Latin homework but anxious about their academic future. Worry is milder and more normative than anxiety, which can become debilitating.

Stress and Pressure

We dive deeply into the distinction between stress and pressure in Chapter 3. For now, think of *stress* as what we feel when the demands of a task or situation exceed our perceived ability to cope. By comparison, *pressure* is what we feel when an important result is on the line and it depends primarily on our performance. For example, a gymnast might feel stressed about not being able to sleep during the all-night train trip to the regional championships but feels pressure that winning the meet depends primarily on them because the team's all-star captain is too sick to compete.

Synonyms for Offspring

Parenting begins long before preschool, but our focus is on school-age children, adolescents, and young adults—people roughly between the ages of three and twenty-three. We use the words *children, kids, youth, youngsters,* and *young people* interchangeably, just for variety and without any prejudice. We occasionally use *teen, teenager,* or *adolescent* when we are making specific reference to twelve- to twenty-year-olds and *student* when we are talking about young people in academic settings. We use gendered terms, such as *son* and *daughter,* sparingly and without any assumptions besides that is how the fictitious character in the anonymized case example identifies themselves. Where specifying a character's genetic sex, gender identity, gender expression, romantic attractions, or sexual attractions is an important element of a fictional case example, we have added these details. Many of the pressures young people experience transcend aspects of their identity; others hinge on aspects of their identity.

Confidentiality

During my three years in Boston, four in Los Angeles, three in Seattle, more than twenty-three at Phillips Exeter Academy, and nearly thirty as a traveling educator for schools and summer camps, I (Chris) have been fortunate to have worked with young people, parents, staff, and faculty from all fifty US states and nearly one hundred countries. I have drawn from those diverse experiences, spanning nearly four decades, to construct realistic case examples for this book. Yes, they are constructed, and yes, they are realistic. Nevertheless, I have always protected the confidentiality of actual persons by constructing aggregates—patchworks of character identities and narrative details that pluck elements from diverse people's stories, across various years, and within multiple settings. In the place of actual identifying information, I have inserted novel demographic information.

Sometimes, I have given names, nationalities, ethnicities, religions, and other characteristics to people in the case examples. I could have chosen to use generic terms, such as *the parent, a child,* and *some culture,* but that would have rendered every example bland and forgettable. The truth—my truth—is that real young people are inspirational and memorable, both in what they have in common and in what sets them apart. I would have done them, and you, a disservice by writing case examples as if identity details did not matter. They do, a great deal. Therefore, I have risked being misunderstood by anyone who chooses to skip these author notes. Thank you for not.

Case Examples

When you read our numerous case examples, remember they are:

1. **Fictitious, but Realistic.** As noted above, all characters and other entities in *The Unlikely Art of Parental Pressure* are fictitious aggregates based on our research and collective clinical experience. Although the concepts accurately reflect elements of the real world, any resemblance to real persons, dead or alive, or to other real-life entities, past or present, is purely coincidental. All references to *school* refer to schools in general, not to specific educational institutions. Our descriptions are fictitious blends that combine realistic characteristics of the hundreds of schools we have visited.

2. **Representing, not Representative.** We have chosen names, settings, and other details that represent many—but not all—dimensions of youth on the six continents where we have worked. In no way are our character sketches intended to stereotype one or more aspects of the identities of any actual person or group. Yes, some stereotypes have a kernel of truth at their core, but our examples are meant to say, "Consider what this interesting parent, child, and setting may represent," not "This parent, child, and setting are representative of others with a similar identity." Conversely, it was not possible to represent elements of every family or individual identity. *The Unlikely Art of Parental Pressure* is but one book, with a finite number of pages, so we hope readers who do not see them-

selves fully represented in our case examples will nevertheless see their struggles honestly reflected in our ideas.

3. **Critical, yet Respectful.** We wrote most of the case examples to illustrate harmful pressure, a major thrust of this book. Therefore, the depiction of parents and children, or their relationship, is not always flattering. Nonetheless, we hope readers remain mindful of our intention: We sought to illustrate the pain and struggles of a wide swath of the global citizenship, not to malign any individual, family, group, country, race, or institution through our depiction of unhealthy thoughts, behaviors, and emotions. As parents, we— Chris and Hank—also struggle, blunder, and strive to do our best. We hold in high regard every person and organization that also strives to raise happy, healthy children.

THE PARENTAL PRESSURE PANDEMIC

It's Bad, but You're Not

L OVING, WELL-INTENTIONED PARENTS FROM ALL OVER THE WORLD are applying unhealthy pressure—the kind that undermines young people's creativity, motivation, emotional well-being, social development, and intellectual curiosity. The push to perform is backfiring. That is the central paradox of parental pressure.

All parents make personal choices about what is best for their child. Beginning with what foods prospective parents should eat to increase fertility and what music to play through the uterine wall after conception to what toys boost IQ after birth and what smartphone plan is most likely to promote parent-child bonding, parents are easily obsessed with their child's development. Fascinating social, ethnic, cultural, educational, political, and spiritual influences are also at play. Not surprisingly, there are thousands of books (including some religious texts) and volumes of academic journal articles that prescribe what parenting style is best for children. To save you time, we have read them all.

OK, we did not read *all* of them. But we did cull through the literature, hunting for fresh ideas, until the books and articles started saying pretty much the same things. Like you, we have sometimes felt confused and exasperated by advice from books, magazines, TV shows, in-laws, bloggers, random advice-givers, and other parents (including our own). Yet a remarkably consistent message emerged from the literature on parental pressure: Parents are applying too much.

This made no sense to us. Why would parents do more and more of something that hurts their child's performance and mental health? Like many anthropologists,[1] we see parents as "rational actors who use their shared knowledge of the world to adapt and make complex decisions in their local community" and who "develop goals and care strategies (i.e., cultural models) that maximize the likelihood that children will attain culturally valued skills and characteristics."[2] Then we realized: Applying pressure is a parental instinct. The popular question *How much pressure is just the right amount?* turns out to be the wrong question.

The Unlikely Art of Parental Pressure swims across the riptide of popular press by focusing on *how* parents apply pressure, not *how much*. And unlike most parenting books, this one will not teach you how to change your kids. It will challenge you to change yourself. Whereas most parenting books take the approach of "Your kid has problems? Then teach them to cope with their feelings and change their behaviors," our approach is radically different and far less authoritarian. We are saying, "Many of kids' problems are relational, which means that both kids *and* parents can contribute to the solution."

In reality, this book is as much about pushing ourselves as parents as it is about pushing our kids in healthy ways. So buckle up. This is hard work. Our suggestions will feel uncomfortable at first because they buck conventional wisdom. We urge you to lean into the discomfort and find bits of gratification in your gradual progress. We also urge you to customize the concepts we present to fit your family's style and traditions. By adopting healthy pressure habits, you can help reduce the profound depression, anxiety, substance abuse, dropouts, and suicides that are caused by unhealthy pressure.

The concept of "pushing your child to be their best self" in our subtitle comes directly from the child-rearing vernacular. Most of us have spoken with a partner, a teacher, or another child's parent about "how hard to push" our child, marveled at how our child knows how to "push my buttons," how we wish our child would "push themselves harder," or how we "feel a certain push" to have our child achieve developmental milestones, such as learning to read. In writing the subtitle, we also wanted to dispel the myth that all forms of parental pressure are harmful. The word *shove* implies malice, the words *make* and *induce* imply coercion, and *press* is something you do to a shirt. Hence, *push*. Done well, it works.

The studies and stories cited in this book bear witness to the predicament parents face as we guide our children toward being their best selves. We apply pressure because we care, but we hinder progress and create problems because of how we apply it. Naturally, learning a new parenting approach takes time. As fellow parents, we are encouraged that you have chosen to read this book. Keep listening to that voice in your head that generously reminds you, *With a modest adjustment today, you can be an even more effective parent tomorrow.* Week by week, your modest adjustments to how you push your child will pay bigger and bigger dividends in their mental health and performance.

Do not equate our encouragement to persevere with the Dodo bird's verdict in *Alice's Adventures in Wonderland.* Asked to judge the winner of a chaotic race, the Dodo exclaimed, "*Everybody* has won and all must have prizes!" Life may sometimes seem like a chaotic race, but not every parenting approach deserves a prize. There is a right way and a wrong way to push your child. Upholding high standards, providing reliable warmth, setting a good example, offering encouragement, granting freedoms to take healthy risks, and coaxing lessons from mistakes are among the most powerful ways to promote positive youth development. By contrast, defining success narrowly and framing the stakes as do-or-die will quickly transform healthy pressure into an interpersonal toxin that diminishes performance, destabilizes emotions, and damages the parent-child relationship.

Beyond this discouraging irony is an uplifting discovery: We parents have the capacity to transform harmful pressure into helpful pressure. Spoiler alert: All parents pressure their children in both harmful and helpful ways at different times. That has always been the case. Only in the last few decades has unhealthy parental pressure become a well-documented crisis. Hence, the goal of *The Unlikely Art of Parental Pressure* is to give parents a healthy road map and a hundred practical tools to ensure that the instinctive pressure they apply to their children promotes development, not distress.

THE ROAD AHEAD

The arc of the book goes like this:

- In Chapter 1, we provide a pair of case examples that illustrate the insidious nature of harmful parental pressure, first from a parent's perspective, then from a child's perspective.
- In Chapter 2, "A Lot in Life," we explain more about the pernicious consequences of the Performance Paradox and its treacherous twin, the Intention Paradox.
- Chapter 3 is titled "Keep Pushing," because—after making a clear distinction between healthy and harmful pressure—we describe how healthy pressure promotes positive youth development.
- We get a little snarky in Chapter 4, "Blame Yourself," knowing that parents take a lot of heat from their kids. We help you get ahead of the curve by explaining the source of parental pressure.
- In Chapter 5, we provide the first of eight practical transformations that liberate parents to shed their Pressure Parent persona and confidently adopt their Support Parent persona.

- Naturally, we could not coin terms without commenting on some pop-culture parenting labels. Chapter 6, "Tigers, Dolphins, and Jellyfish," will bring clarity to your parenting self-assessment.
- Chapters 7–12 provide six more practical transformations that will help solidify your Support Parent persona. We use stories, tables, and research to illustrate the healthy side of competition, emotional expression, empathy, listening, praise, criticism, questions, and parental involvement.
- In Chapter 13, "Open Your Mind and Your Heart," we explain how harmful parental pressure intersects with corrosive social and cultural pressures. Our eighth and final suggested transformation outlines how parents can help thwart this damaging combination.
- In the last chapter, "Push with Prowess," we offer additional guidance to complement our eight transformations. You will learn more about helping your child perform under pressure as we wax philosophical about parental pressure and other caregiving ideals worth striving for.
- Our epilogue is an appeal to parents and professional educators. Although higher education is just one source of harmful pressure, it is both potent and changeable. With parental support, professional educators may be able to lead by example and inspire healthy change in other pressurized subcultures, such as neighborhoods, corporations, and high-achieving schools.

※

Nowhere in *The Unlikely Art of Parental Pressure* do we suggest that parents stop pushing. Quite the opposite, in fact. We endorse the balanced pressure that parents apply when they combine high standards, reasonable rules, and unconditional love with the freedom for kids to make some of their own decisions, falter, and learn from mistakes. We tout the loving pressure that parents infuse with empathy and compassion. We encourage the honest pressure that arises from effective praise, criticism, and questions. And we implore parents to fight against racial, ethnic, cultural, identity, peer, social, and economic pressures—pernicious pressures not of their doing but whose undoing depends on their love.

Give yourself credit for all the wonderful ways you have parented your child. Realizing that you may have laid on some harmful pressure means that you are human. Have some humility, but do not beat yourself up. The pandemic of pressure is bad; you are not.

Finally, as you move through these chapters, remember that *how* matters much more than *how much*.

chapter one

GLORIA AND LIZ

Parental Pressure from Two Perspectives

R EGARDLESS OF THEIR AGE, ALL CHILDREN NEED AT LEAST ONE WARM, reliable adult to believe in them and provide comfort, especially in times of distress. Most parents remember a time when their child came to them upset. A classic example might be the complaint, "I hate school and I have so much homework that I'll never get to do anything fun this weekend." Most parents also remember a time when they responded to their child's distress with sage advice, such as, "Yeah, well, school is important, so let's take a look at your assignments and see what you should work on first." And finally, most parents remember a time when their child threw that supportive bid back in their face with some version of "Don't tell me what to do!" or "Stop lecturing me!" or "You just don't understand!" What is going on? Parents are trying to help, but kids are rejecting the offers. We think, *What do you mean I don't understand? I understand quite a bit, which is why I'm giving you great suggestions!*

What explains this frustrating disconnect? Perspective. Parents and children often see the same problem quite differently. In this example, the child—be they in second grade or sophomore year—wants empathy. They want the parent to feel their pain, to acknowledge their dismay. By contrast, the parent—who has seen this all before—wants the child to solve the problem quickly, before things get worse. However, putting problem-solving before empathy is a recipe for conflict, as we will discuss in Chapter 10. For now, just appreciate how different a parent's perspective can be from the child's, as well as how unexpected the impact can be, regardless of the parent's intentions. Pressure is more complicated than a heavy night of homework, but it is also experienced differently by parents and children. Consider the case example of Gloria and Liz, a mother-daughter pair whose relationship and personal well-being have been ravaged by unhealthy pressure.

GLORIA—MOTHER, AGE FORTY-FOUR

Gloria is married, but tonight she feels like a single mom. Her husband, Abel, is away again on business, hard at work in a different time zone. Their daughter, Liz, is also far from home and hard at work. She is studying and running track at an independent school, somewhere in a third time zone, and feeling tremendous parental pressure. Hang on. With the family so dispersed, how could parental pressure be an issue?

Looking at the time on her phone, Gloria realizes that she needs to work efficiently because Liz is probably already awake. Gloria wants Liz to have a fantastic day, so she feels compelled to complete one more task this evening before going to bed. The lights are off in the kitchen, but the city glow through the kitchen window is enough for her to see the table and chairs. She sits down and taps the space bar on her laptop, kindling a second source of glowing light.

Using Liz's username and password, Gloria logs in to the student portal of the school's website. The virtual private network (VPN) she pays for allows reliable access to foreign websites. This premium VPN also anonymizes Gloria's computer IP address and encrypts her keystrokes, routing her access through a server on a distant continent. Unbeknownst to Gloria, Liz is walking to an appointment on that same distant continent with vague thoughts of suicide slowing her pace.

On the laptop screen, a tiny animated graphic chases its own tail to indicate that the website browser is waiting for a response. Gloria removes her glasses to rub her eyes. *We've been preparing Liz for almost seventeen years to get where we are now,* she thinks. *I guess I can wait thirty seconds for the student portal to load.* She misses Liz, as loving parents do when their children are away from home. She reminisces about the Saturday afternoon she told her husband that she was pregnant. *This child is our life now,* she had said to Abel. *We'll both have to work even harder.* Since that day, they have devoted the bulk of their time, salaries, and Saturdays to Liz's education, with a singular goal for her: to succeed. They believe that if Liz can outshine her high school classmates in one or more ways, her chances of collegiate success—and ultimately professional and financial success—will improve dramatically.

When Liz was in elementary school, Gloria would leave work to pick her up after school and drive her to a private math and English tutoring center staffed by the local university. After tutoring, Liz and her best friend would walk the two blocks to their figure skating lesson, after which one of Liz's parents would pick her up on their way home from work. When he was not on a business trip, Abel would help Liz with her homework while Gloria prepared a homemade lunch for their daughter to carry to school the next day. On most days, with Abel away, Gloria was both tutor and cook.

The laptop beeps, and Gloria's attention snaps back to her research. She repositions her glasses as the familiar landing page resolves. Even before the global spread of deadly viruses that necessitated online learning, most schools had purchased learning management systems (LMSs)—software that made it simple for teachers to upload digital course content, take attendance, and post grades. Gloria knows from experience where to find the My Courses section of this LMS. She inhales, blows a quick sigh of anticipation, and clicks Biology 410. The next page lists assignments and test grades for the course over which Liz has poured the most sweat and shed the most tears. Her current grade is a B+. Any score over 94 on yesterday's exam would boost her to an A–. Gloria finds the number in the column labeled Exam Three: 91.

Gloria studies the number, knowing that it will not raise Liz's course grade into the A range. However, the online syllabus lists three more graded assignments. There is reason to hope. And to strategize. By most standards, 91 out of 100 is an outstanding grade. Unless, of course, most of Liz's classmates scored in the high 90s. In that case, 91 is relatively low. Too low, in all probability, to make Liz's final grade stand out. Unless . . .

Gloria touches an app on her phone that opens a list of individual and group contacts. She finds what she's looking for near the top of the screen. This group chat, comprised of parents whose kids attend the same school and are poised to graduate in the same year, is also a silent measurement tool, a kind of rough probability calculator. She posts this message to the group:

> Bio 410 still a grind for Liz. So much memorization! Yesterday's test = 91.

The absence of an adjective to describe Liz's numerical grade is a subtle way to tempt other parents—mostly moms—to share their child's grades on the third exam; one way to learn how Liz's academic achievement stacks up against that of her classmates; one way to decide whether some of the family's disposable income should be spent on a biology tutor; and one way to refine Gloria and Abel's calculation of their child's chances of being admitted to a top university next year. One thirteen-word post in one group chat could harvest responses that will influence Gloria's emotions, the parents' investments, the family's social status, and the direction of Liz's education.

EXTREME OR EXTREMELY RATIONAL?

You may think that Gloria's motives and methods are extreme. Yet when it comes to our children, we all want the best, and we are willing to make sacrifices to provide what is best. Perhaps Gloria's behavior is rational, but the *circumstances* are extreme. Of course, rational is not always right. In 2019, the FBI's Operation Varsity Blues exposed thirty-three parents who had paid more than $25 million between 2011 and 2018 to William Rick Singer, head of the Edge College & Career Network. Singer had used some of the millions to falsely inflate students' standardized test scores, fabricate some of their achievements, and bribe college coaches and officials to arrange to have the children of the thirty-three coconspirators admitted to top colleges and universities in the United States.[1] Few parents have the wealth to write checks for hundreds of thousands of dollars, and even fewer would leverage their privilege to bribe a school to admit their child. Yet the fact that some did attests to the pressure that many parents, in many parts of the world, feel today. This pressure—to give one's child an advantage in an increasingly competitive and populated world, to acquire bragging rights about the prestige and selectivity of certain schools—has become the social-emotional pandemic of our time.

The American Psychological Association's news magazine, the *Monitor,* recently featured an article on the increased student self-referrals to college and university health centers for anxiety and depression. The story summarized research that validated what clinicians in secondary and postsecondary schools have been saying for decades: Student mental health is getting worse at alarming rates.[2] The clinicians in counseling and psychological services at high schools and universities across the country get more referrals than they can easily handle.

In an earlier press release, the APA summarized findings from a Harris Poll survey of 1,018 adolescents and 1,950 adults in the US. The two groups were roughly equivalent in what they perceived to be a healthy level of stress: 3.9 out of 10 for teens and 3.6 out of 10 for adults. However, the teens' self-reported stress levels during the school year—5.8 out of 10—far exceeded what they perceived to be healthy levels. During the summer, levels were lower—4.6 out of 10—but still unhealthy. According to the study, "Many teens also report feeling overwhelmed (31 percent) and depressed or sad (30 percent) as a result of stress. More than one-third of teens report fatigue or feeling tired (36 percent) and nearly one-quarter of teens (23 percent) report skipping a meal due to stress."[3] Follow-up studies in the APA's *Stress in America* series have found that political discord, racial injustice, and the COVID-19 pandemic have all increased self-reported levels of stress.

To expand on the definition of stress we provided in the authors' notes at the start of this book, let us consider the origins of stress. The source of stress can sometimes be *extrinsic* (coming from outside the person, such as from a parent or an upcoming exam) and can sometimes be *intrinsic* (coming from within the person, such as from ruminating about the worst thing that could happen). Just as stress can be a force exerted on objects (like a load of heavy, wet snow bending a tree branch), stress can also be a force exerted on people (like a load of difficult courses straining a student's ability to keep up).

OK, but why is stress increasing among young people? If human stress is a state of physical, mental, and/or emotional strain or tension resulting from adverse or highly demanding circumstances, then we have to ask: Are we giving kids more difficult tasks than before? Or is task difficulty unchanged and kids' coping abilities have taken a nosedive? Is it possible that tasks and abilities are both unchanged, but kids are misperceiving how hard life is and/or how well they can cope? All three of these factors have probably contributed a bit to the increased stress levels that young people report, even before the COVID-19 pandemic.[4] We are here to report on a fourth factor: parents. Loving, well-intentioned parents.

PARENTS AS SOURCES

Stress has many sources and can take many forms, but the evidence suggests that none matches the emotional intensity of parental pressure. A recent study from Penn State University showed that out of 421 students (227 females and 194 males), 19.4 percent had contemplated suicide because of the enormous pressure from their parents to produce exceptional grades.[5] Ironically, research conducted by the Pew Research Center suggested that the majority of American adults (56 percent) felt that parents put *too little* pressure on students.[6] Just 15 percent felt that parents put *too much* pressure on students. However, adults in China, India, and Japan reported the inverse perceptions: 63 percent, 61 percent, and 59 percent of adults surveyed in those countries, respectively, felt that parents put *too much* pressure on students.

Whatever cultural differences exist in the perception and application of parental pressure, the actual harm to young people across the globe is undeniable. In response to heightened awareness of the intense pressure young people report, creative journalists and licensed mental health professionals have shared wholesome ways of coping with academic, athletic, artistic, and social stress—both online and in print. However, none has offered suggestions for preventing parental pressure in the first place. We believe that is because it cannot be prevented. We also believe that the problem will worsen until parents understand why parental pressure is inevitable and commit to transforming harmful pressure into healthy pressure.

Parents apply pressure because they care. No blog post, focus group, or scientific survey will ever change that. Moreover, parents themselves are under a great deal of pressure, both personally and professionally. Most of us also judge ourselves—and feel judged by others—according to how well our children are doing. For their part, mental health providers and professional educators continue to debate what constitutes the "right amount" of pressure. Nothing has changed all that. Until now.

The Unlikely Art of Parental Pressure is a clarion call to stop blaming parents for doing what comes naturally and to stop asking the wrong question. Forget "How *much* parental pressure is too much?" We owe it to our children and ourselves to start asking, "What *kind* of parental pressure is healthy?" and the related question: "How can parents *transform* harmful pressure into healthy pressure?" The answers are fascinating, hopeful, and practical. If you are motivated to change, even a little bit, then this book is for you.

Gloria's story offers a glimpse of a parent under pressure. She has devoted herself to her daughter and immersed herself in Liz's academic life. Her commitment may be excessive, but, so far, it is hard to see how Gloria's behavior has made Liz suicidal. To understand the harm, we need to see things from the child's perspective. We need to know what the pressure put on Liz by her parents feels like.

LIZ—STUDENT, AGE SIXTEEN

After months of coping on her own, Liz self-referred to Counseling & Psychological Services for what she describes to me as the "double whammy" she faces: "*I'm* freaking out trying to pull As in all my classes, but if my parents knew that I was seeing a psychologist, *they* would freak out. Right now, I could be using this free period to study bio or practice Tchaikovsky. Plus, you know that mental health problems—any problems, really—are juicy gossip for the other moms." Liz pauses. "I guess that turns out to be a triple whammy, not a double. Now you know why I think about dying, Dr. Thurber."

When I ask how it is possible for other students' parents to know that she is seeing a therapist, Liz looks at me quizzically. "Through apps, Dr. Thurber. Apps."

For years, I have known that the moment children enroll—from preschool to prep school to university—parents flock to smartphone messenger apps to start comparing notes on their children's experiences. In Asia, Africa, and South America, most parents are on WhatsApp. In China, Korea, and Japan, the dominant apps are WeChat, Kakao Talk, and Line, respectively. Parents in North America, Australia, and Europe are split between Facebook Messenger and WhatsApp, with English-speaking parents taking to Facebook pages and Instagram (owned by Facebook), often to brag about their progeny but in a less organized way than on any of the dedicated messenger apps. All of this happens quickly. For example, on December 13, 2018, Harvard University notified the 935 early-action applicants to whom it had offered admission from a pool of 6,958. By the next day, the private Facebook group Parents of the Harvard Class of 2023 was live and quickly grew to 490 members.

Parents' preferred platforms vary, but the apparent purposes of these online communities has remained constant: lighthearted social support and the casual sharing of school information. The reality is that when Liz confides in her mom that she received a 98 on a calculus test, her mom shares her grade with the other parents in the group chat within seconds. Low scores, of course, are typically not shared—a practice that aligns perfectly with the worldwide custom of curating our virtual lives in a way that amplifies accomplishments.

The real peril results from Liz's mother having the password to her account on the school's student portal and/or its LMS. For most students, it feels only mildly controlling to have their parents know what the homework is and when it is due. Grades are different, at least at this age. Consciously or unconsciously, many parents feel that grades reflect performance and performance reflects talent. Talent can get you into a top-tier school, and top-tier schools are international symbols of prestige, both at the secondary and postsecondary level. Of course, prestige carries weight in some circles, but it never carries the day. How did pride in our kids become more about which *school's* name is on the diploma than which *student's* name is on the diploma?

. . . .

LIZ SIGHS AND RAISES HER EYEBROWS. "MY MOM KNOWS when I have a test coming up, of course. A day after the test, she gets online, like every half hour or something, to see my grade as soon as the teacher posts it. Half the time—and this is just one of the crazy parts, Dr. Thurber—other parents and students know my grade on a test before I do."

"Your mom's getting on a messenger app and posting your grade in a parent group or two, even before you have a chance to see it yourself," I say, trying to summarize and understand at the same time.

"Exactly. Well, sometimes she just posts that I did really well but leaves out the number. Either way, a lot of those moms are then telling their own kids what I got, or that I did well or something, even though it's technically none of their business."

"Not even technically. Ethically." I try to be empathic without sounding too surprised or judgmental.

"I don't know what's worse," Liz continues, "the fact that other kids are coming up to me, all snarky, like, 'Oh, so you got an A− on that last math test. What did you miss?' or, like, the fact that these other kids get crap from their parents like, 'I heard so-and-so got an A. You could get As, too, if you studied harder. Maybe we shouldn't have sent you to that expensive school in the first place.'"

Liz's voice sounds softer now and a bit distant. "No wonder half my friends are suicidal. They're working their asses off—sorry—getting like four hours of sleep a night, and the people who are supposed to be their main supports are telling them, 'You're not working hard enough' or 'You're not worth the money' or 'You bring shame to this family.'"

"You're getting pressure from all directions: your parents, other kids, your teachers, and yourself," I say, starting to feel helpless. "They make you feel ashamed sometimes."

"Lots of kids get pressure from parents. That I can handle, even when they threaten to pull me out of school if I get Bs. I'm sure you've heard that before, Dr. Thurber. You know, like, 'We're not paying this crazy

tuition for you to get Bs and then go to some no-name university.'"
Liz looks up at me, and I can see that her eyes are getting teary. She
continues, "But what's really messed up is that I feel pressure from this
kind of . . . competition . . . or comparison . . . with other kids that is
totally parent-generated."

"And your parents make it seem like there's just one prize worth winning," I say.

"Obviously," replies Liz. "It's like if I don't get admitted to this or
that school—and you know which ones we're talking about, Dr.
Thurber—I'm a total failure. Why go on?"

"It's probably hard to concentrate and do your best academic work
when the definition of success is so narrow and the stakes are so high."
I think about how unlikely it would be for her parents to withdraw her
for B-range grades, but her fear that they would is her reality.

"Welcome to my world," Liz says with an ironic grin. She leans her head
back and opens her eyes wide to prevent the escape of welling tears.

"Well, I'm glad you're here," I say. "It's a lot to handle, and I can see how
the circumstances change your feelings about school . . . and yourself.
And your parents, too, I guess."

When I point out that our meetings are not only confidential but also
free (i.e., included in every student's yearly Health Services fee), Liz protests. "They track my phone, Dr. Thurber. They'll know I'm here in the
Health Center. Don't worry. I've thought this all through. I can just lie
and tell them that I had a cold or something." Anticipating my next
question, Liz adds, "And no, I can't just turn my phone off or they'll get
even more suspicious."

For Liz, the parental pressure is not only explicit and authoritarian but
made worse both by the rapid and public comparisons to peers and
by her stellar achievement to date.

"You don't know what it's like," Liz says. "The better I do, the more anxious I get that I won't do as well the next term or even on the next test.
Even my college counselor said to me, at the end of last year, 'Congrat-
ulations on your 94 average. Just don't let that drop or the admissions

committees will wonder what's wrong.' Speaking of which, I have to study for Latin. Is it OK if we meet for just thirty minutes?"

I make a trite comparison to a roller coaster, attempting to capture her emotions in a colorful metaphor. "No," Liz objects. "A roller coaster goes up and down and eventually stops. I'm on a rocket that keeps accelerating. Not only can't I get off, I don't know when it's going to disintegrate because it's exceeded the tolerances it was built for."

. . . .

In the remainder of our session, I assess Liz's mood. The chronic stress and unhealthy pressure she has been feeling has created some classic symptoms of depression: sadness, loss of interest and pleasure in activities that used to bring joy, low energy, low intrinsic motivation, difficulty concentrating, appetite changes, and insomnia. She looks exhausted, but she never sleeps through classes. In fact, her attendance and academic performance have been excellent, which explains why her adviser and teachers have not suspected she was seriously depressed. Even her three close friends—two in the boardinghouse and one at the school newspaper offices—are unaware, or at least have not expressed concern. And although Liz shares with me that she sometimes thinks life is not worth living, she has no intention of hurting or killing herself. Nevertheless, I double-check that she understands how to contact the counselor on call, suggest some healthy ways of coping, and am pleased that she agrees to another meeting.

chapter two

A LOT IN LIFE

Two Parenting Paradoxes

B EFORE DAWN, JUST A FEW DAYS BEFORE YOU PICKED UP THIS BOOK, four smartphone alarms jolted four parents awake.

In Los Angeles, California, thirteen-year-old Jacob's father woke him up to shower and eat half a protein bar before playing through the first movement of Brahms's second piano concerto and uploading the recording to his teacher in Stockholm, Sweden.

In the suburbs of Berlin, Germany, eleven-year-old Bruno's father woke him up and stuffed two bagged meals into his rucksack before Bruno caught the bus to the third round of the Junior Olympics diving team tryouts.

In downtown Shenzhen, China, eight-year-old Jinsu's mother woke her up to study English flash cards before eating a breakfast of *zhou* (rice porridge) and walking to school with her grandmother.

And in Delhi, India, sixteen-year-old Poonam had already been awake for twenty-five minutes when her mother knocked and opened the door to the bedroom she shared with her sister. The glow from Poonam's laptop gave her face a ghostly hue and exaggerated the bags under her eyes when she glanced up. Her mother smiled as Poonam's gaze returned to the screen and the videoconference with her American college admissions consultant.

Every morning, parents all over the world wake up and get their kids going. Many of those children and teenagers have the luxury of going to school. Others, less fortunate, go to work to help their families. The least privileged go out looking for food, some without the benefit of parents or surrogate caregivers to help launch the day. A few young people go searching for the next adult who might toss a coin in their cup or pay them to perform a service, no matter how degrading or dangerous.

As with their homes, cultures, and caregivers, the pressure that kids feel varies enormously. The pressure to fill the void in one's stomach and the pressure to fill the void in one's résumé are worlds apart. Yet common to all youth is their need to feel loved. Indeed, kids will do almost anything to appear competent, to seem worthy of attention and affection, especially in the eyes of parents. For this reason, parental pressure is uniquely potent.

Young people's instinctive craving and striving for parental love is rivaled only by parents' drive to protect their young. Together, these forces forge intergenerational bonds that are essential to the survival of the species. Millennia ago, children who lacked value in their parents' eyes were abandoned and often perished. Even today, in some subcultures, children who lack worth to parents are suffering physical abuse, sexual abuse, and even murder.[1] Compared to prostitution, honor-based violence, and mob executions, unhealthy parental pressure seems paltry but can also be lethal. Around the globe, children who lack worth to parents—or who feel that way—are succumbing emotionally. Their instinctive craving and striving for parental approval makes those young people especially vulnerable to parental pressure.

We parents also feel a biologically pre-wired pressure. We strive to max-imize our offspring's chances for survival and success. That is laudable, at least when it comes to survival, which is easy to define. Success is much harder to define because it is fueled by concerns about the future (which is full of unknowns) and distorted by quirks in the culture (which we shape, sometimes unintentionally). Therefore, whether parental pressure hurts or helps depends partly on how an individual parent defines success.

As parents, we periodically revise our definitions of success, often to bring them back into alignment with our values. For example, when the head coach of our boys' sports team started using harsh and arbitrary discipline, I (Chris) sat down with my wife and our boys to discuss what was happening. Together, we decided to wrap up that program at the end of the season and devote more time to music—both instrument practice and participation in the boys' school band and orchestra. We chose not to define success as a first-place trophy and not to let happiness or civility be the price of success. Decisions like these are highly personal, and the options available to different families vary tremendously. Therefore, we have intentionally refrained from being prescriptive. (Well, at least we have tried not to be too heavy-handed.) Let your family's values and options shape your definition of success, and let your heart shape how you communicate that definition to your child. Then let the subsequent chapters in this book shape how you apply the pressure it takes to achieve that success.

For too long, well-intentioned parents have unwittingly undermined their children's functioning by defining success in narrow, do-or-die terms. Instilling this high-stakes mindset is just the start of harmful paren-tal pressure. When combined with other forms of harmful pressure, par-ents' limited, high-stakes definitions of success can drive young people to the point of panic, despair, hopelessness, and even suicide. This seems especially true for academic success. Although the thoughts and feelings that motivate completed suicides are never certain, school counselors believe family conflict and academic pressure—both of which increased in 2020 during the COVID-19 quarantine—are two main causes.[2]

PERNICIOUS PARADOXES

How exactly are parents defining success in narrow, do-or-die ways? Consider the four early risers we introduced at the start of this chapter. Jacob must not simply compete in the concerto competition, he must win it. Bruno must not simply make the diving team, he must captain it and compete in the Olympics. Jinsu must not simply pass her English test, she must attain a perfect score. And Poonam must not simply get accepted to college somewhere in the US, she must be admitted to an Ivy League university, Stanford, or MIT.

Not surprisingly, when complete success or complete ruin are the only options in a young person's mind, mental health and performance worsen. In other words, the notion of a "clutch play"—wherein extreme pressure catapults a person's skills from excellent to superior—is a myth.[3] We call this the **Performance Paradox**.

We can all remember that goal, ace, basket, checkmate, home run, penalty kick, bluffing bet, or touchdown pass that won the championship in the final seconds. Yet these dramatic moments are the exceptions, not the rule. High drama, in the form of perceived high stakes, actually impairs performance.[4] Add a layer of guilt—generated by parents' recounting how disadvantaged their childhoods were, or by their reciting the litany of sacrifices they made to get their child "this far"—and the perceived stakes become even higher. Paradoxically, motivation and achievement decline in such circumstances.

The treacherous twin of the Performance Paradox is the **Intention Paradox**. In this case, the myth many parents believe is that intention and impact are identical. In other words, if a parent applies pressure with the intention of helping their child, then the impact of that pressure will be to help. Yet that is not always the case. Paradoxically, many of the adults who care most about their child's survival and success, who say they consistently apply intense pressure because they know and want "what is best" for their child, are the very same adults who erode the connections they are seeking to nurture. Add a layer of conditionality—where parents describe their love and support as contingent on a specific, high-stakes outcome—and the parent-child relationship is further weakened.

If you are feeling crummy right now, take heart. The Performance Paradox and the Intention Paradox are surmountable. Nurturing is what we parents do best, which is why we are the most powerful antidote to harmful pressure. In discussions with our children, we can intentionally describe success as multifaceted, while simultaneously upholding high standards. We can love our children unconditionally while helping them learn from failure. And we can struggle against toxic cultural tides to raise happy, healthy children (who, by the way, must be capable of thwarting pernicious influences by themselves one day).

By identifying when and why all parents sometimes lapse into **Pressure Parent** mode, we can avoid the next tempting opportunity to narrow the definition of success, to exaggerate the cost of failure, or to hinge our affection on achievement. Of course, improving our parenting skills is easier said than done. As parents, our lot is a lot. Fortunately, we have thousands and thousands of chances to get it right. (We recommend you adopt this last sentence as a meditational mantra.)

Each day, you can have a go at parenting your child in an even healthier way than you did yesterday. Each day brings new opportunities to express warmth and empathy, shape realistically high expectations, set a kind example, praise genuine effort, teach self-reliance, encourage creativity, model humble learning from mistakes, nurture autonomy, and ask whether your parenting style is amplifying or assuaging the unhealthy social and cultural pressures our kids get from sources outside the family system.

That sounds like an outrageously lofty list of parenting skills, but only because we assembled them in a single list. The steps to making a peanut butter and jelly sandwich sound equally imposing if we list them all together. Would you doubt your culinary abilities if we wrote: Each day brings new opportunities to purchase a fresh and hearty loaf of bread; to slice off two pieces with a sharp, serrated knife; to ensure that the pieces are thick enough to prevent jam seepage but not so thick they make the sandwich dry; to spread your favorite peanut butter (or soy-nut butter— your call) on one slice of bread; to spread jam evenly on the other (but with a separate knife so that you don't cross-contaminate); to carefully bring the peanut butter slice and the jam slice together, pressing hard enough to form a bond but not so hard that you begin extruding peanut butter, jam, or both; and, finally, to slice the completed sandwich diagonally with the same serrated knife you used at the start.

Do you feel motivated to embark on such an epic? It sounds complex and laborious, not like something people enjoy performing every day. Many things sound complex and laborious at the start. But when you experience some early successes and enjoy the instant benefits, you will feel motivated to continue. Learning to apply healthy pressure is just like that.

chapter three

KEEP PUSHING

Healthy Pressure vs. Harmful Pressure

FOR PARENTS SEEKING TO RESOLVE THE TWIN PARADOXES OF PAREN-tal pressure—the Performance Paradox and the Intention Paradox—the first essential step is: *Keep pushing*.

Nope. That's not a typo. Applying pressure is important to every child's healthy development, provided that it is healthy pressure, not harmful pressure. In this chapter, we will explain that distinction, starting with **Figure 1**. In the next chapter, we will describe our new model of parental pressure, which serves as the basis for all the insights and practical tips in subsequent chapters.

In our research and clinical practices, we have witnessed at least seven dimensions of parental pressure that bear down on children: Importance, Opportunity, Competition, Perfection, Urgency, Control, and Display. These dimensions overlap, but we have separated them in our diagram so we can discuss the difference between two parenting personae—the **Pressure Parent** and its inverse, the **Support Parent**. Before we describe

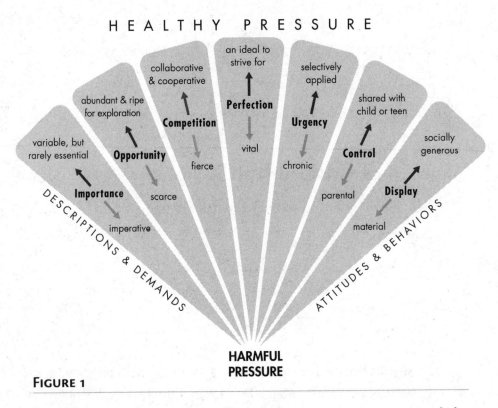

HEALTHY PRESSURE

an ideal to
strive for

collaborative
& cooperative

Perfection

selectively
applied

abundant & ripe
for exploration

Competition

Urgency

shared with
child or teen

variable, but
rarely essential

Opportunity

vital

chronic

Control

socially
generous

DESCRIPTIONS & DEMANDS

Importance

scarce

fierce

parental

Display

ATTITUDES & BEHAVIORS

imperative

material

**HARMFUL
PRESSURE**

FIGURE 1

these different approaches to parenting, it is important to expand the distinction between *pressure* and *stress* that we introduced in the authors' notes, just before the introduction. (Gold star if you read those two sections already. Bonus points if you go back and read them now.)

STRESS = DEMANDS > RESOURCES

When the demands of a situation exceed our resources, we experience stress. For example, if you estimate that completing a writing assignment will take at least two hours but the assignment is due in just one hour, then you will feel stress. Stress is the experience of *There is no way I can get this all done.* We feel beset and overwhelmed. We wish we had more time, more skill, more money, more teamwork, or more of some other resource to meet the demands of a task. That's stress.

PRESSURE = PRECISE, HIGH-STAKES OUTCOME + PEAK PERFORMANCE

By comparison, when the stakes are high and a low probability or narrowly defined outcome hangs on our best performance, we experience pressure.[1] For example, if the referee sets you up for a penalty kick in overtime of the championship match, you feel pressure. Pressure is the experience of *Success depends on my performance in this high-stakes moment.* We feel anxious or fearful. We wish that the stakes were lower or that the outcome did not hinge so directly on our peak performance. That's pressure.

HAVING VS. USING

Another way to look at the distinction between stress and pressure is that stress is about *having* what it takes; pressure is *using* what it takes, especially when it really counts. We typically feel stress *in the lead-up* to an event, wondering whether we have what it takes; we feel pressure *during* the event itself, wondering whether we can deliver the goods and carry the day. When you reference "the moment of truth," or a "make-it-or-break-it," or a "do-or-die" circumstance, you are talking about pressure. In other words, pressure moments are the stressful moments that are *super important* to us.

Consider the elements of stress and pressure in this case example:

"SHE'S FRICKIN' CRAZY," GENEVIEVE SAID, BEFORE SHE EVEN sat down to begin our seventh session. "Look at this!" She angled her smartphone's screen toward my face. I stepped closer to read the texts, but she just handed me her phone as we neared our seats. "Go ahead, Dr. Thurber," she challenged like a quarterback who had just lateraled the football to the fullback. "Scroll through that." I began to read.

[Mom] Your father stiffed me again, that bastard.

[Genevieve] why u telling me this?

I don't know who's gonna pay your tuition bill.

want me to text him?

It's not your problem.

u just made it my prob

Hahaha

seriously . . . what are we gonna do?

I'll worry about your father. You focus on school. Junior year is the most important for college.

how can I focus on school when my parents are at war?

We're not at war. We're divorced.

same

Same what?

nothing

You're bitter because I didn't call on your birthday. I get it. I said I was sorry. You have no idea how busy things are here. I meant to call. I called you first thing today, remember?

how could I forget? still dark out when u called

How do you expect me to react when you are so ungrateful?

how do u expect ME to do well in school when I don't get enough sleep?

You're not there to sleep until noon, damn it! You're there to get into a decent college. But don't think we're going to keep paying your tuition if your grades keep dropping.

#newsflash

So if you know how important it is to do your homework and get to class, then why don't you?

I glanced up. "Wow," I said in a low tone, handing the phone back.

Genevieve narrowed her eyes and studied me. "No," she said. "*Wow* would be like: *Your mom called on your birthday and balled you out for getting a B in math.*" She paused. "That, I could handle. But my mom didn't even call me on my birthday because she was too busy battling her ex-husband—my ex-father—over the tuition bill. That's frickin' crazy, like I said."

. . . .

For students like Genevieve, **stress** comes from doubting whether she has or can acquire the resources (money, in this case) to meet the demands of the situation (the tuition bill, in this case). Stress also comes from abstract instances of demands exceeding resources, such as doubting whether her parents have the priorities and diplomatic skills to resolve their differences, or whether Genevieve herself has the time and energy to endure her parents' bitter conflict.

By comparison, **pressure** comes from feeling that certain high-stakes outcomes—such as staying in school and receiving financial aid—depend on Genevieve's stellar performance—namely, top grades and near-perfect attendance. Whether her parents would *actually* require her to withdraw because of a falling GPA and a growing collection of unexcused absences is beside the point. What Genevieve *believes* is what intensifies the perceived pressure.

PRESSURE PARENTS AND SUPPORT PARENTS

How human beings *experience* both stress and pressure depends largely on how we *think* about the demands placed on us, about our skills and resources, and about how high the stakes are. For most early humans, survival itself was a daily source of stress. Their bodies demanded food, water, and shelter from the elements, but those resources were not always available, the skills for acquiring them not always highly developed. Therefore, many early humans probably experienced a high baseline level of chronic stress. Moreover, because their hunter-gatherer existence depended on peak performance in key moments, the do-or-die context transformed their stress into pressure. Uncomfortable, high-stakes pressure moments were common for early humans.

For many modern humans, there are fewer high-pressure survival moments, but they still exist. In the last century, military conflicts, climate changes, and diseases have caused food shortages and famines. Even without wars and pandemics, gathering food may still involve financial strain, transportation inconveniences, logistic challenges, and irregularities in supplies—perhaps all four. Fortunately, gathering food is less likely to be a life-or-death circumstance for modern families than it was forty thousand years ago. Between 75 and 90 percent of children living in upper-middle-income and high-income countries can find a snack in the fridge, look in the cupboard, or wait until dinner.[2] However, that means that even in the wealthiest countries, between 10 and 25 percent of young people will not be exaggerating when they say, "I'm starving." The modern equivalent of "If I can't find something to eat soon, my life may end" is one of the highest-pressure circumstances there is.

Keep these and other objective differences in children's lives in mind as you progress through this book. As well, keep in mind that how people *experience* stress and pressure depends largely on how they *think*. And how people think, especially when they are young, depends heavily on how parents describe the world.[3]

When we adopt a **Pressure Parent** persona, we describe a world that exists in the narrow, pointy ends of the fan diagram at the start of this chapter. It is an urgent, competitive world, controlled by parents who demand perfection and who delight in broadcasting their children's prestigious achievements, regardless of how much help they received.

As for its effects on children, think of those same pointy ends in **Figure 1** as concentrated forces, like the tips of high-heeled shoes. If your dancing partner is wearing stiletto heels and steps on your foot, it will hurt much more than if they were wearing tennis shoes. Why, exactly? Because the stiletto heels concentrate the forces induced by your partner's weight and movement onto a small area: the bottom tip of the shoe's high heel. Flat-soled tennis shoes, on the other hand, distribute these same forces over a larger area. It still would not feel good to have someone wearing tennis shoes step on your foot while dancing, but the pain and risk of injury would be far less. The pressures depicted in the HARMFUL PRESSURE tips of our fan diagram are like the forces exerted by a stiletto heel: concentrated, uncomfortable, and likely to cause injury.

By contrast, when we adopt a **Support Parent** persona, we describe a world that exists in the broad ends of the fan diagram. It is a collaborative world of hard work and high standards, where parents praise prosocial behavior and challenge their children to take age-appropriate initiative, find new opportunities, and stay true to their core values as they develop self-reliance.

All of us have applied healthy pressure and unhealthy pressure to our children. At times, we adopt the Pressure Parent persona by describing a world to our children where opportunities are scarce, competition is fierce, tasks are many and urgent, and perfection is essential for success. The more we control our children's behavior by setting precise goals, narrowing the criteria for success, and flaunting their accomplishments, the more we adopt our **Pressure Parent** persona.

When we adopt our **Support Parent** persona, however, we describe a world where opportunities are as abundant as a child's willingness to explore and where collaboration is personally and socially beneficial. In this world of healthy pressure, few tasks are inherently urgent, and most worthwhile tasks require patience and sustained diligence. Support Parents describe perfection as an elusive, individualized ideal, used to set goals and motivate striving, not as a litmus test of their child's worth. In the healthy pressure world, Support Parents also embrace failure as integral to learning and praise efforts more than outcomes.

Here are some samples of how parents act and sound when they inhabit the opposite ends of the seven pressure categories in **Figure 1**. These brief examples might not sound like you, but they capture the essential contrasts between what Pressure Parents and Support Parents say. When you actually speak to your child, think about where you put your emphasis, and use your own words to make it sound natural.

IMPORTANCE

Pressure Parent

"Yes, you need to rewrite this thank-you note! Look—your printing is messy, it's way too short, and you haven't personalized it at all. This is your one and only chance to distinguish yourself from the other kids who interviewed for this job."

Support Parent

"When I get a thank-you note, it feels more meaningful when the
handwriting is neat and the person mentions something
specific that they are grateful for. You could make a more
positive impression if you took the time to rewrite this."

OPPORTUNITY

Pressure Parent

"There are just a few universities with international reputations.
Unless you get into one of them, no one will care where
you went to school or what you did there. It won't help you
get a job. Success is all about reputation and pedigree."

Support Parent

"Ivy League schools have international reputations for a reason, but
there are other great schools out there. In the end, what
you accomplish at school is far more important than its
reputation. Success is about attitude and innovation."

COMPETITION

Pressure Parent

"Get in there and practice! If you want to make the team, you have
to be better than the other kids who try out. I promise
you that none of them is playing video games right now
because they're hungry to beat you out for a spot."

Support Parent

"Getting better takes time and concentration. If you feel bored
practicing alone, try calling one of your friends who is also
trying out for the team. I'm sure you can help each other
and improve both of your chances of making the team."

PERFECTION

Pressure Parent

"I don't care whether you like this ice or not, you have to skate perfectly today if you want any of these recruiters to notice you. You have to be fast, precise, and strong. If you're not ready to deliver 110 percent, let's pack up and go home."

Support Parent

"I know that every time you go out on the ice—no matter what it feels like—you try your best. Let these recruiters see how ambitious you are; let them see you striving to be faster, more precise, and stronger than ever."

URGENCY

Pressure Parent

"Get in the car right now! We're going to be late! Why is it that no one in this family is ever on time for anything? I've told you a thousand times to prepare your backpack the night before. But do you ever listen? Never!"

Support Parent

"We should have left already. Let's work together quickly to gather everything we need before we go. And next time you have a lesson on Saturday morning, I'll remind you to prepare your backpack on Friday night. I know you can do better."

CONTROL

Pressure Parent

"I know that the idea of summer camp seems fun, but you're not the one paying for your education. I am. That means I'll

decide what is most important for your future and right
now . . . that's not camp. You're taking an SAT course."

Support Parent

"Let's think together about your summer. I know summer camp
would be a fun option. You and I also talked about
preparing for the SAT. Why don't you research both
options, including the cost, and we'll discuss a plan after
dinner."

DISPLAY

Pressure Parent

"If you wear the blue blazer, you'll look like every other student
coming for an interview. That's why you're wearing the
Italian wool. With a fitted shirt, a silk tie, and your cap-toe
Oxfords, it will be obvious what sets you apart."

Support Parent

"In your interview, be sure to talk about the work you did outside of
school. They're not just looking for someone with original
ideas, they also want someone who takes initiative and
contributes to the community."

If reading these contrasting examples made you feel annoyed or
dismissive, you may be spending more time as a Pressure Parent than
you realize. Maybe not. What is important is that you have now become
more mindful of seven common channels for parental pressure, and you
have begun to internalize the difference between healthy and harmful
pressure.

Pressure Parent? Support Parent? Really? Why add one more set of
modish labels to the popular parenting lexicon? Because the current
pandemic of Pressure Parenting has proved to be unhealthy, counter-

productive, and even deadly, for our children. The more we behave as Support Parents, the healthier, happier, and higher-achieving our children will be. Now is the perfect moment to examine your current parenting practices and start adjusting your style in ways that will most benefit your child.

In the next chapter, we will describe our model of parental pressure, so you can better understand the source from which these seven blades of pressure emanate. Like most sources of psychological energy, we can refine or redirect them once we understand them. Certain elements can prove resistant to change, yet all are worth analyzing in our journey to become more mindful, intentional, and effective parents.

chapter four

BLAME YOURSELF

Where Parental Pressure Starts

BLAME YOURSELF? FOR REAL? WELL, IF YOU DON'T, YOUR KID WILL. Someday anyway, if they have not already. You did it when you were younger. We all did, at some point. It's normal. But just because it *is* normal does not mean it is completely true. Some of the pressure our children complain about is simply because they are . . . well . . . our children. Every generation of children, stretching back millennia, has found fault in their parents and, in the next breath, vowed to do better if they become parents. So we have to take the heat, *and* we have to put this inescapable censure into perspective.

Sometime in late childhood, we all become aware of our parents' flaws. That's normal. Then in adolescence, those flaws become the sparks that inspire snarky comments and ignite major conflicts about how to parent. That's normal too. Then in early adulthood, we swear that we will never repeat our own parents' mistakes, if we become parents ourselves. Also normal. Naive, maybe, but normal.

If you have ever admonished your child with something like "Darn right you're going to practice. We didn't pay for an instrument and lessons so you could play for a few months and then quit," then you have probably also looked over your shoulder to see whether one of your own parents said it. Rare is the parent who has not flinched while whispering, *I promised myself I'd never say that.* All parents deserve credit if they possess the humility to admit they have justified themselves to their disobedient or ungrateful children (that's all children, at least some of the time) with the classic, *Because I said so!*

These realizations are reason to smile, knowing that all children will flinch for the same reason and justify themselves in the same way if they become parents. An even bigger reason to smile is the fact that children also feel grateful for the ways parents support them, love them, and, yes, pressure them. We acknowledge that some readers have experienced trauma at the hands of a parent—trauma that may overshadow positive memories of support, love, and healthy pressure. If this describes you, we hope there nevertheless exists gratitude for at least one trusted adult from your youth. Our points are that even the most loving caregivers have flaws, even the most difficult children have goodness in their hearts, and all but the most painful parent-child relationships have pieces to appreciate.

Whatever mixed memories and emotions you feel about the parenting you received, you clearly care about parental skill building because you are holding this book in your hands. Most parents of most animal species also have something else in common: They possess an instinct to protect their young; to ensure their survival. In many religious traditions, this is a commandment from a divine power. From an evolutionary viewpoint, this is a genetic trait, selected for over many generations, to ensure the propagation of our genes. Whether viewed from a spiritual or scientific perspective, the parental instinct to protect our young is an indisputable truth. Because every parent starts with this protective drive, our model also starts there.

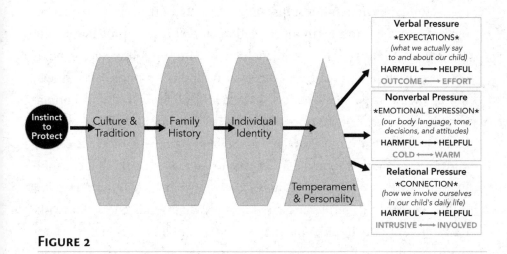

FIGURE 2

What happens next is characteristically human. The energy to protect is magnified or diminished through three lenses—Culture & Tradition, Family History, and Individual Identity—before passing through
the prism of Temperament & Personality and taking one of three basic
forms: Verbal Pressure, Nonverbal Pressure, and Relational Pressure.
Figure 2 illustrates this theoretical flow of parenting energy.

Like the fan diagram in the previous chapter, **Figure 2** is an oversimpli-
fication. The driving force that fuels parental pressure is not really a light
that shines through a series of lenses and determines how parental pressure
looks, sounds, and feels to our kids. Although the four lenses are symbolic,
the influences of culture, tradition, family history, individual identity, temperament, and personality on *how* parents apply pressure are real.

Moreover, just as real glass lenses are made of compounds consisting
of different chemical elements, our four metaphoric lenses contain different psychosocial elements. Some of these elements are primarily positive
and some are primarily negative; others can go either way. For example,
the **Culture & Tradition** lens could include not only cuisine, language,
and music but also institutional oppression, racism, and sexism, not to
mention religion, art, and attire. The **Family History** lens could include

race, ethnicity, and relationships; violence, addiction, and psychopathology; and perhaps immigration, education, and choice of profession. The **Individual Identity** lens could include not only intelligence, gender, and sexual attractions but also personal prejudice, trauma, and illness, not to mention personal beliefs, habits, and preferred ways of coping. Finally, the prism of **Temperament & Personality** includes a parent's emotional reactivity and characteristic style of expressing themselves. We chose a prism rather than a convex lens to indicate that these factors are like firmware in a parent's brain—somewhat shaped by environmental influences, but primarily hardwired in a way that sends energy in markedly different directions. A parent's temperament and personality refract the waves shining through the other lenses, giving the expression of parental pressure a style that is uniquely characteristic of that individual parent and more or less consistent with their emotional reactivity and self-expression in non-parenting contexts.

There is no exact science to quantifying all these factors. (Remember, that is precisely why the word *art* is in the book's title.) **Figure 2** is shorthand. To say that human behavior is complex is a laughable understatement. (Do not write that on your psychology final exam.) However, our point is simple: Being mindful of the influences depicted in **Figure 2** is the prerequisite to refocusing those influences in a way that improves our parenting and benefits our children.

Consider this case example:

• •

Santosh's father answers on the first ring. I identify myself, reassure him that there is no emergency, then ask whether he has a few minutes to talk about his son. "Go right ahead," he instructs in flawless English, colored with his Mangalore accent. I dive in, being careful not to blame. "Dr. Gadad, I'm concerned about the pressure Santosh perceives. In fact, sometimes he—"

"I should hope so!" the father interjects. "While the rest of the world's gardens grow weeds, I'm busy tending to mine. I am upholding a certain standard here, Dr. Thurber. I know, as his parent, that Santosh is capable of straight As. He knows it, even as a teenager. And now you know it. His mother and I have very high expectations for him, just as our parents had for us. With top marks, he'll get into a top university. He needs to make something of himself, you know."

"Every parent wants—" I start, but the father continues.

"These are realistic expectations, Dr. Thurber. We all need someone to believe in us. You're a psychologist. You know that, don't you? Without our expression of confidence, as his parents, where would Santosh be?"

The father's question hangs in the silence before I reply. "I definitely support high standards," I proffer, "but sometimes I worry that the expression of those standards backfires because they are so very high or because kids feel that there is only one specific, acceptable outcome... and the stakes seem really high. I just worry that Santosh feels—"

"We care what Santosh *does*, not so much about what he *feels*," Dr. Gadad interrupts. "There are parts of every child's education that they dislike. Everyone knows this. Nobody said it would be easy. It certainly wasn't for me. Or for Santosh's mother. And right now, we are concerned that Santosh is frittering away his education. When I spoke with him last night, I made it perfectly clear what we expect. And that's that, Doctor."

· · · · · · · · · · · · · · · ·

To some readers, this parent's goals and methods may be unreasonable or even incomprehensible, but plugging the data into our model provides some clarity. Like all parents, Dr. Gadad starts on the left side of **Figure 2** with an instinct to protect his child. He describes the cultural lens through which he looks with the statement, "While the rest of the world's gardens grow weeds, I'm busy tending to mine." He describes his family history lens with the statement, "Nobody said it would be easy. It certainly wasn't for me." He reveals something about his temperament and personality with each of his interruptions and minor condescension. We can also surmise that multiple factors have shaped this parent's individual identity: his own educational achievement, the premium he puts on achievement over emotion, and his authoritarian attitude. By the time his instinctive drive is expressed, all the way on the right side of **Figure 2**, the verbal result is to tell Santosh that he must get As to get into a top university. And although one cannot discern body language from a phone call, some of the father's attitudes and decisions do shine through. The relational result seems to be conditional affection. (Clinical and advisory conversations with Santosh had indeed revealed that he felt most of his parents' approval hinged on achieving a nearly perfect GPA.)

Without knowing more, we must also allow for the possibility that Mr. Gadad is angry because he believes Santosh is not trying hard enough. If Santosh truly has been wasting lots of time gaming, vaping, or procrastinating, then his father's disappointment is understandable, his tone reasonable. However, from the information we have, this appears to be a classic example of Pressure Parenting. Dr. Gadad has portrayed college admission as a rare, competitive, urgent matter that requires Santosh's immediate, superior performance. For his part, Santosh is likely to perceive his current situation as both high stakes and narrowly dependent on immediate peak performance. As we described in Chapter 1, this is likely to have the paradoxical effect of *lowering* Santosh's motivation, *diminishing* his performance, *depressing* his mood, and *weakening* his relationship with his parents.

Surprisingly, some children and adolescents whose parents apply harmful pressure *do* excel—sometimes academically, sometimes athletically, sometimes artistically. If you cannot think of some domain where harmful pressure seemed to boost performance for your child, you might be able to think of an example from another family. With this example in mind, it is tempting to believe that harmful pressure works as well as, if not better than, healthy pressure. Yet that is a mistaken belief, albeit common. Thinking that harmful pressure works well is an error in thinking called *the availability heuristic*. Humans often use one salient example to draw conclusions about how the world works.

The availability heuristic is like having one old relative or distant friend who loves to smoke but has not yet developed emphysema or cancer. It is tempting to think, *Smoking actually isn't that bad.* By generalizing that one salient example, we are overlooking three less visible points: (1) Smoking has damaged that person's body in lots of ways that we cannot see. The only data that are available are the smiles on Aunt Betty's face when she uses the butt of one cigarette to light the next one. (2) A sample size of one person is not representative of the larger population. Aunt Betty may be an outlier, in the sense that most people who smoke as much as she does, for as long as she has, are dead. (3) Just because two things sometimes happen together (correlation) does not mean that one is making the other happen (causation).

Back to parental pressure. It is true that peak performance sometimes follows harmful pressure, but false that the two are directly related. Whenever young people excel *despite* harmful pressure, there is always a step in between, a kind of moderating variable. To end in peak performance, unhealthy parental pressure must pass through an in-between stage where the child transforms it in one of two ways. One adaptive transformation is to become passionate about the activity (e.g., studying, practicing, acting a certain way) or enamored by the activity's long-term result (e.g., admission, winning, social advancement). In turn, this passion creates motivation, perseverance, and, ultimately, peak performance. Children who perform extremely well *despite* heaps of harmful pressure have found a way to graft the source of pressure from their parents to themselves and a way to ignore their parents and, as the saying goes, keep their eyes on the prize.

Take Nina, for example. Her parents force her to practice the piano for three hours each day, and they make her participate in several concerto competitions each year, hoping that a collection of first-place performances will distinguish Nina from other high school seniors when it is time to apply to college. Nina might hate it all, feel miserable, fight with her parents, and start shoplifting from the local mall. It would be easy to look at a case like Nina's and blame the effects of unhealthy pressure. But what if we saw the opposite? What if Nina coped with her parents' harmful pressure by transforming it into a love of music, a passion for performing, and an obsession for competing with other young musicians? Or what if Nina transformed her experience of harmful pressure into an appealing fantasy of becoming a famous musician? It would be easy, however misguided, to conclude that her parents' intense pressure was the direct cause of her good mental health and excellent piano playing. In fact, the real story would be how artfully Nina transplanted the source of pressure from her parents to herself.

Another way children can adapt to harmful parental pressure is to decide that the only way to escape is by appropriating their parents' fantasy for their future or by adopting a mindset of *I can endure this until I'm eighteen.* This cognitive dodging allows some children to endure extreme parental pressure and appear to be motivated to perform at an elite level of sports, arts, or academics. However, this usually comes at a great cost to their mental health. Fearful perseverance makes children resentful, anxious, and depressed. It rarely makes them love the activity their parents are forcing them to do, and usually ends in quitting. Feeling obligated to perform is suffocating. Worst of all, chronic coercion damages the adult-child relationship.

Dr. Gadad, from the example earlier in this chapter, is doing his level best to ensure his child's success. However, his application of unhealthy pressure is likely to backfire. If he wanted to take a different approach, to assume a supportive posture, he could begin by praising Santosh for all the things his son is doing well. Next, he could provide some genuine empathy by saying something like, "Juggling multiple commitments is always difficult." Then, he could ask some open-ended questions, such as, "When you are doing well in a course, what are you actually doing that helps you learn?" followed by, "How can you do that more often?" or "How can you apply what you know about how you learn best to *this* course?" Notice how these questions start from a place of strength: Santosh often does well at school.

This type of empathy and appreciative inquiry would likely make Santosh feel less pressure and more connection to his father because he would feel understood and optimistic. In that calmer and more motivated mindset, Santosh—like every human being—would have an easier time figuring out how to improve.

There are so many possible reasons for lower-than-expected academic performance: an obnoxious roommate, a video game addiction, difficult coursework, or a disorganized teacher, to name a few. Thus, the simple demands of "work harder" or "get As" have no effect. By comparison, patiently and collaboratively looking into the different factors that are causing higher or lower grades in certain classes can point to strategies that actually improve performance. Not only does this supportive approach *feel* better, it also *teaches* better. A central goal of parenting should be to impart this kind of strategic wisdom on our children. At its core, the pressure *we feel*, as parents, is not really about a particular academic course, athletic event, or artistic competition. It is about wanting our children to thrive as adults, even after we are not around to support them.

As dreamy as that honorable goal sounds, it is easy to forget. Sometimes, the disappointment or anger we feel when we witness our children underperforming can hijack our reasoning and strap us into our Pressure Parent persona. We object. We demand. We criticize. We do not bother searching for the causes of their underperformance. And by commanding a better outcome and connecting that outcome to a narrow definition of success, we are simply ramping up the pressure and failing to teach our kids *how* to be successful. To repeat something like, "You'd better start improving your game stats this season if you expect to be recruited to a D1 school in a couple of years. There's no other way you're getting in," will ultimately impair a child's athletic performance, intrinsic motivation, and mental health.

We cannot measure successful parenting solely by our child's achievements. Sure, we can be hugely proud, but we should measure success by how well we have helped our children create sustainable systems of persistent effort, honesty, self-awareness, kindness toward others, and healthy ways of coping with life's ups and downs. We should also measure success by how intrinsically motivated our children are to achieve peak performance. Someday, of course, we will not be around, so it would be foolish for any parent to be the only (extrinsic) source of motivation. By adopting the ideas and applying the techniques in this book, you will create a sustainable system within your child that allows them, over a lifetime, to put forth great effort and achieve great things in whatever intellectual, artistic, athletic, and interpersonal paths they pursue.

In **Figure 2**, you can see that when your instinct to protect refracts out of the **Temperament & Personality** prism, it shows up in one of three ways: Verbal, Nonverbal, and Relational. And this energy can harm or help your child, depending on whether you are in Pressure Parent or Support Parent mode. In the next few chapters, we explain how adopting a Support Parent persona can transform a cold, intrusive focus on outcomes into a warm, involved focus on effort. We will show you how realistic expectations, consistent warmth, and reliable relationships weave a web of support that improves your child's performance and strengthens their character. As a bonus, **Transformation 1** provides you and your child with greater happiness than you could have ever achieved from applying prolonged, harmful pressure.

Rather than blaming their parents, children of Support Parents make their beds each morning, complete their homework each night, brush their teeth twice a day, get along with siblings and peers, and always eat their vegetables.

OK, that last paragraph is baloney. But all the other stuff in this chapter is true. You might still get blamed for something, but at least now you can say that you knew what you were doing and you knew it would help.

chapter five

EXPECT *THEIR* BEST, NOT *THE* BEST

How to Spark Interest and Nurture Motivation

• TRANSFORMATION 1 •

LUCA'S FATHER LEANS OVER THE GRANDSTAND RAILING TO WHISPER in his ear. "You can see the leaderboard," he says. Luca listens as he adjusts his wrist straps. "You're a tenth of a point behind first place," the father continues. "You need at least a 9.0 on this final event to win your age group and really go somewhere with your gymnastics. High bar is your best event, so I need you to stick the landing."

Across the gym, Luca's rival, Abeo, is also getting a pep talk from his father. "I'm impressed, Son," the father says as Abeo adjusts his wrist straps. "Your concentration and effort have earned you two personal bests today. Now give it everything you've got on this final event. Work hard to stay focused, especially during your kip. High bar is your best event, so let's see you stick the landing."

Notice how differently these two fathers try to psych up their boys. Luca's father's stated expectation (verbal pressure) is for Luca to come in first place at this gymnastics meet. He is also clear about his personal investment when he says to Luca, "I *need* you to stick the landing." Taking a different approach, Abeo's father's stated expectation is for Abeo to keep doing his personal best. Abeo still feels pressure, but his father's investment is more collaborative, which you can hear when he says to Abeo, "*Let's* see you stick the landing." At first, these may seem like small differences, but how we state our expectations to our children has an enormous effect on their motivation. Luca's father's focus is on the outcome; Abeo's father's is on the effort. Both parents love their sons, and both parents mean well. Both have invested time and money in their child's athletic performance. And both boys feel the normal pressures of competition. But all other things being equal, only one boy got a pep talk that will make a positive difference; the other boy is feeling a wave of unhealthy pressure that is likely to impair his performance.

EXPECTATIONS AND OUTCOMES

Clearly stated expectations help children succeed in life, but as with other forms of pressure, their harm or effectiveness depends on *how* parents state their expectations. In a classic study of the power of expectations, Harvard professor Robert Rosenthal and school principal Lenore Jacobson arranged for teachers in a California primary school to administer a brief intelligence test to their students in grades 1–6 at the start of the 1964 academic year.[1] The researchers had hypothesized that many teachers, probably without realizing it, would behave more positively toward students they believed to be the most intelligent and promising, compared to students they believed to be less capable. In turn, this positive treatment, driven by teachers' high expectations, would have a positive effect on students' performance.

After teachers administered the intelligence tests, the researchers scored them but did not share individual students' test results.[2] Instead, they told the teachers that some of their students appeared to show "unusual potential for intellectual gains" and casually gave the teachers the names of those students. In truth, there was no difference between the average test scores of the students on the "unusual potential" list and the students not on the list. The researchers had just randomly selected 20 percent of the 255 students to be on that list.

Eight months later, near the end of the academic year, students retook the test. Comparing their May scores to their September scores revealed that students in first and second grade whom the researchers had randomly identified as intellectual bloomers had, on average, made larger gains than had the other children. Rosenthal and Jacobson speculated that teachers had manifested their expectations as more positive behavior toward the "unusual potential" students, such as using a warm tone or praising their creativity. In other words, teachers' expectations had become a self-fulfilling prophecy. The researchers also speculated that the effect of teacher expectations on students' test scores was strongest in the youngest students, because their self-concept was most susceptible to teachers' treatment. However, when all the students were given the same intelligence test one year later (i.e., twenty months after the initial test administration), "the greatest gains were among the children who had been in the fifth grade when the 'spurters' [unusual potential students] were designated and who by the time of the final test were completing sixth grade."[3]

Although Rosenthal and Jacobson did not record teachers' classroom behavior, they did ask the teachers to think back over the entire school year and comment on their students' classroom behaviors. The analysis of these retrospective reports suggested "the children from whom intellectual growth was expected were described [by the teachers] as having a better chance of being successful in later life and as being happier, more curious and more interesting than the other children."[4] Despite the limitations of its design, this study sparked hundreds of methodologically rigorous studies of how teachers' expectations influence student performance. More than fifty years later, Rosenthal and Jacobson's broad conclusion endures: teachers' positive expectations are associated with student growth. The effect seems more robust for boys[5] and for students of majority ethnicity. Conversely, teachers' negative expectations tend to slow student growth.

To any parent who has complained that their child "just won't listen," Rosenthal and Jacobson's study (as well as subsequent studies with similar results) is a reminder that children *do* listen (and feel and notice). They may not always do exactly what we ask them to do, but they hear what we expect. Our words, our tone, our facial expressions, and our other interactions with them—especially when they form a reliable pattern—communicate powerful messages about what we expect. In turn, those messages change the course of children's development. Their self-concept, mood, motivation, and performance improve or decline based on our expectations and on how we express them.

Looking back at Mr. Distasio (the father whose stated expectation for his son, Luca, was *to win*) and Mr. Oroyinka (the father whose stated expectation for his son, Abeo, was *to try his best*), you might wonder: What's wrong with telling Luca that he has to win? That is the same as telling him that he has tremendous promise as a gymnast, right? Wrong. Stating the requirement to win is different from stating the potential to win. Outcomes-based expectations usually backfire, whereas effort-based expectations usually help. Here is why:

In the Rosenthal and Jacobson study, the students themselves were not told anything. The researchers gave the *teachers* information on which students were likely to be intellectual bloomers. In turn, the teachers unwittingly treated those students differently; they treated those students *as if they had great promise*. The teachers never demanded a specific outcome from those students, such as, "You need to score 130 or higher on your IQ test at the end of this academic year." Instead, the teachers were warmly supportive of those students, which appeared to have motivated those students to engage their intellects more. The teachers subtly expressed their expectations of success. And as a result, those students' cognitive abilities increased, at least as measured by the *Tests of General Ability* (TOGA, 1960).

When parents focus on specific, narrow outcomes, such as scores, awards, and rankings, they add three unhealthy layers: competitiveness, perfectionism, and fragility. What would have been healthy competition becomes a cutthroat rivalry. What would have been high standards of achievement become an unreachable set of flawless ideals. And what would have been resilient self-esteem becomes a brittle self-concept.

WHEN PRESSURE BACKFIRES

When a parent repeatedly tells a young person that beating their peers is the ultimate achievement, that young person is likely to develop unhealthy competitive behaviors, such as cheating, plagiarism, and poor sportsmanship. When a parent tells a young person that 1,600 is the only worthy score on the SAT, that A* is the only worthy score on the GCSEs, or that 670+ is the only worthy score on the *gaokao*, that student risks becoming so perfectionistic that anything less feels devastating. And when a parent tells a young person that success is synonymous with the name of a school, the color of a ribbon, or the size of a bank account, that child's self-esteem can become so fragile that they lash out when they fall short. Consider this case example:

· ·

JAKE'S FATHER WAS AN ALUMNUS OF A TOP UNIVERSITY AND had told Jake from the time he was in primary school that he was destined to enroll at that same university when he graduated from high school. "Every other university is a safety school in my dad's eyes," Jake remarked wryly during the winter of his senior year.

A month later, when his father's alma mater sent Jake a rejection email, Jake lashed out by calling the university and anonymously reporting that a classmate, whom the university had accepted, had failed to disclose a prior disciplinary infraction. The university admissions committee had no choice but to call the boys' high school and verify the truth of this report.

As it turned out, the admitted peer had indeed lied on his application by checking the NO box on the Common App question "Have you ever been found responsible for a disciplinary violation at any educational institution . . . ?" As a result, the university revoked the acceptance of Jake's classmate, citing both dishonesty and concerns about the nature of the disciplinary event, which involved illicit substances.

At the same time, the high school launched its own investigation into the identity of the anonymous caller. Although Jake's confession in psychotherapy was, by law, confidential, it did not take long for the high school's deans to form a list of likely suspects. When directly questioned by a dean, Jake admitted his foul play and faced his own major discipline case. In the therapy sessions that followed his confession, Jake expressed both relief and regret. It took weeks of tearful reflection for him to understand the internal and external forces that had compelled him to sabotage his classmate and, at the same time, throw his own college process into disarray.

· · · · · · · · · · · · · · · ·

Jake had been admitted to several excellent universities at the time of his fateful phone call, but the college counseling office's policy required that Jake notify those schools about his misconduct and subsequent requirement to withdraw from school. As a result, two universities rescinded his admission, and one deferred its offer for a year, contingent on Jake's receiving additional psychotherapy and then submitting a petition describing his personal growth. Jake never earned a high school diploma, but because he had completed all the required coursework and credits for public high school, he received an equivalency certificate in the state where he lived.

For Jake, as with so many young people, parental expectations turn poisonous when they connect worldly success and personal worth to a highly specific and ambitious outcome. It was a classic do-or-die scenario. In Jake's mind, both his father's approval and his self-concept hinged on admission to a single university—one that is perennially ranked among the top ten in the world. Besides luck, the way to boost his chances for admission would have been by trying his best throughout high school. But where would the motivation for such sustained diligence come from?

To answer this question about drive, we first need to return to **Figure 2** in Chapter 4. Jake's father begins with an **Instinct to Protect**, which all parents possess from the moment their child is born or adopted. Like all instincts, it is hardwired and evolutionarily beneficial. Of course, Jake is thousands of years removed from needing to do his best to gather food, escape predators, or find a mate. In modern times, parents instinctively know that their children will have an easier time earning a living someday if they get a good education, formal or otherwise.

Pressure from the Instinct to Protect then passes through the lens of **Culture & Tradition**. The Western culture in which Jake's father grew up attaches great status to diplomas from top universities. It assumes that such a diploma is a proxy for having learned useful facts, made valuable connections, and practiced beneficial strategies for modern-day survival. Also in this lens are cultural assumptions that people without college diplomas are less smart, or less capable, or less employable, compared to those with diplomas. In addition, Jake's father was educated in a traditional Western way, with the standard progression of primary and secondary school leading to a four-year degree from an accredited university, rather than to an apprenticeship or vocational school.

Next, the pressure passes through the lens of **Family History**. Perhaps the father's own parents were fixated—as many parents are—with their son's having "a better life" than they did. Or perhaps Jake's father feels a strong positive association between having graduated from university and having pleased his own parents. Maybe Jake's grandfather was a graduate of the same prestigious university, and everyone wants Jake to continue the tradition. Or perhaps Jake's grandmother makes delicious meals whenever the family gathers to watch the university's football team play their rival team. There could be a dozen emotional associations—some obvious, others subtle—that Jake's father formed growing up in his particular family.

Next, the pressure passes through the lens of the father's **Individual Identity**. Perhaps Jake's father remains competitive, athletic, or fiercely loyal, so that every time the neighbor wears a sweatshirt from the rival school, Jake's father jokingly shouts, "Safety school!" over the fence. Jake may have come to believe that his father would look down on his attending another university, taking a gap year, or blazing his own nontraditional educational path. Or maybe Jake's father once told him that he would teach him "the secret handshake" if he were admitted to his dad's alma mater. Harmful pressure can be so subtle that it seeps into parent-child relationships unnoticed, masquerades as privilege, or both.

Finally, the pressure refracts through the prism of **Temperament and Personality**. Perhaps the father's expressiveness, extroversion, and pride make him more likely to mention his alma mater in casual conversation than would a reticent, introverted, and modest parent. The result may be that Jake gradually becomes aware of his father's expectations.

The particulars of Jake's relationship with his father and other caregivers, his perception of their professional accomplishments, Jake's siblings' (if he had them) attitudes, the family's socioeconomic level, and other dimensions get complicated. Fortunately, most of the research on the effects of parental expectations and pressure has looked at these family variables. In the domains of academic and extracurricular achievement, the results are striking.

THE HEAVEN AND HELL OF EXPECTATIONS

First, the good news. Many studies of primary- and secondary-school students have found the same positive effect of expectations that Rosenthal and Jacobson discovered. Parents who express high expectations for achievement are more likely to have high-achieving children, compared to parents who express low expectations.[6] In fact, parental expectations for children's academic achievement predict educational outcomes better than actual parental involvement, such as attending school events,[7] (which not all parents can do anyway, depending on circumstances). Parental expectations are a powerful predictor because they change not only how kids think about their aptitude and their future but also how parents treat them. For example, parents with high academic expectations talk more about school with their kids than do parents with low academic expectations.[8] Parents with high educational aspirations for their children also provide more out-of-school learning opportunities for their children.[9]

Parental expectations also affect the child's own aspirations and expectations. For instance, some studies suggest that parents' expectations for their children's academic attainment have a moderate to strong influence on students' own goals for postsecondary education.[10] For their part, students who reported that their parents expected them to attend university had better attendance and more positive attitudes toward school, compared to students whose parents did not expect them to attend university.[11] As you would guess, these beneficial effects of explicit expectations depend on *how* parents communicate them.

Now, the bad news. When parents express expectations with an intense emphasis on high achievement or perfection, kids tend to have low self-esteem, engage in delinquent behavior, and feel pessimistic about achieving the goals their parents set for them. Unintentionally, parents crush interest in the very activities parents *want* their kids to dominate. The paradoxical and self-destructive consequences of parents' intense emphasis on achievement or perfection seem especially true for affluent adolescents, who have both the access—such as cars they can use—and the means—namely, money—to engage in certain kinds of unhealthy risk-taking, such as alcohol and other drugs.[12]

Related research with affluent families found that when parents were perfectionistic, adolescents tended to feel intense pressure to compete for top spots, as well as to develop social, emotional, and behavioral problems.[13] However, activities with peers may dilute the negative effects of parental perfectionism. Those teens who joined organized activities, such as a softball team or a robotics club, were able to cope in healthier ways with their perfectionistic parents than teens who did not participate. Perhaps the recreational, less formal nature of these organized, shared activities gave those teens some welcome relief from feeling that they had to be perfect. Or perhaps being part of a group made them feel as if the responsibility for achievement was no longer theirs alone. Or perhaps some teens took a long-term view and chose to endure some lackluster activity (if indeed that is how they saw it), knowing that someday it would be an asset to their résumé. As you read in Chapter 4, some young people can transform unhealthy parental pressure into an adaptive motivator. Over time, however, even these kids end up unhappy.

Pressure Parents who think they can keep applying intense pressure— hoping their child will someday transform that noxious force into something healthy—are likely to make an unpleasant discovery. Not only are highly pressured kids at risk for mental health problems and underachievement, but there is also no way to predict which exceptional children can temporarily convert intense external pressure from parents into self-motivation. A far more reliable way for parents to ensure healthy development and optimal outcomes for their kids is to adopt what psychologists call an *authoritative* style of caregiving. As we will explain in the next chapter, an authoritative style balances control (which provides boundaries and guidance) and warmth (which provides love and understanding) to help kids feel good and be their best selves.

chapter six

TIGERS, DOLPHINS, AND JELLYFISH

How Parenting Style Predicts
Children's Adjustment

I N 1969, CHILD PSYCHOLOGIST HAIM GINOTT WROTE ABOUT TEENS
who said their parents would "hover over them like a helicopter."[1]
Since the publication of Ginott's *Between Parent & Teenager*, the list of
labels for parents of a certain ilk has expanded beyond *helicopter parent*
(over-involved) to include *tiger parent* (obsessed with achievement) and
lawnmower, snowplow, or *bulldozer parent* (driven to remove obstacles to
their child's achievement).

Journalists and bloggers have also popularized labels for various
parenting extremes. In contrast to tiger parents, *elephant parents* are
excessively nurturing and protective. When parents emphasize prolonged physical closeness, such as co-sleeping through age five, they
are known as *attachment parents*, and when they go with the flow, by
de-emphasizing rules and expectations, they are *jellyfish parents*. As a
throwback to their own childhoods, parents who allow their children to

explore the neighborhood or ride the bus by themselves are *free-range parents*. And—sticking with the zoological theme—*dolphin parents* balance these extremes by collaborating with their children, having reasonable rules and expectations, being firm yet flexible, and partnering with their community (the rest of the pod) to nurture their child's nature.

Social scientists have also sought to categorize caregivers. The most durable modern classification of parenting styles was published in 1967 by developmental psychologist Diana Baumrind, then at the University of California–Berkeley.[2] Later expanded from three parenting styles to eight by Baumrind herself in 1971 and then consolidated to four in 1983 by Stanford University's Eleanor E. Maccoby and John A. Martin,[3] this sorting method is most often depicted along perpendicular axes of Control and Warmth, or what Baumrind called Demandingness and Responsiveness. We are fond of Graeme Stuart's infographic, reproduced here as **Figure 3**, because his synonyms and catchphrases help to capture the essence of the four parenting styles and because it shows how the dimensions of Responsiveness/Warmth and Demandingness/Control vary along a continuum from Low to High. As you can see, this body of research codifies parenting styles into **Permissive**, **Authoritative**, **Uninvolved**, and **Authoritarian**.

Although Baumrind studied mostly white, middle-class preschoolers and their mostly heterosexual parents in Berkeley, California, more than four hundred subsequent studies have replicated and refined her results with youth of different ethnicities and socioeconomic levels, as well as with parents of different sexual attractions and marital statuses. In a rare convergence of pop culture and science, it turns out that many trendy labels, such as jellyfish parents, *do* have some validity. For example, researchers have been referring to Permissive parenting for more than half a century, long before the label *jellyfish* appeared in print.

But why care about all these descriptions? Surely, parents have been offering commentary on other parents' styles for millennia. The answer is: **outcomes**. Parenting style matters because each category in **Figure 3**

FIGURE 3

is reliably associated with different outcomes. And outcomes matter—to both parents and children—across all cultures, ethnicities, ages, and social classes. (A quick note: When we say, "parenting style" or "category," from this point on, we are referring to the four quadrants in **Figure 3**. These categories are grounded in research. Other labels may sell magazines and earn web page clicks, but they lack ecological validity.)

Parenting-Style Effects

As we previewed at the end of Chapter 5, researchers have repeatedly found that parents who primarily use an **Authoritative** style have children who are generally well-behaved, happy, academically successful, socially skilled, and self-confident. You guessed the rest of the punch line. The outcomes for the other parenting styles are less favorable. **Authoritarian** parenting is associated with children who have higher rates of substance use and delinquency, poorer mental health and social skills, and lower self-esteem and academic performance. Children of **Permissive** parents tend to be more impulsive and selfish, have poorer social skills, and struggle with relationships. **Uninvolved** parenting is also associated with impulsivity, as well as with delinquency and substance abuse. Not surprisingly, the offspring of uninvolved (or neglectful) parents also have the poorest mental health outcomes, including the highest rates of suicide.

Before you panic, recalling that evening when you neglected to help your child with their science project—probably because you had to fix a leaky faucet, attend a meeting, or work late—pause to remember what you know from experience: Real parenting does not exist in neat quadrants. Moreover, consider the secret most researchers do not talk about, especially if they themselves have children: All parents spend at least a little bit of time in all four quadrants of **Figure 3**, every week if not every day. Here is what that might sound like:

. . . .

CHELSEA IS AN ANNOYING TEN-YEAR-OLD. ACTUALLY, SHE IS adorable, but her parents—Stu and Barb—feel annoyed by what they perceive to be Chelsea's chronic dawdling. No matter how much warning they give her, she is never ready on time. Sometimes, she puts on and takes off five different shirts before choosing a favorite; other times, she can't find one of her shoes. At least once a week, she misplaces her homework. As a result, her parents are often late driving her to the bus and must drive her all the way to school. Sometimes, those extra miles and minutes make them late to work.

Depending on their mood, their work obligations, Chelsea's attitude, and even the weather, Stu and Barb respond to her chronic morning dillydallying in different ways.

Possible Response 1: AUTHORITATIVE

parenting style: *high warmth / high demandingness*

typical qualities: *responsive, high expectations, democratic*

Before backing up her laptop and files, Barb stops in Chelsea's room to check her progress.

"Chelsea, you're not dressed yet, and Dad's got breakfast ready. What needs to happen in the next five minutes for you to be on time for school today? Do you need my help picking a shirt or packing your backpack? We're all leaving the house at 7:20, so let's get moving."

Possible Response 2: AUTHORITARIAN

parenting style: *low warmth / high demandingness*

typical qualities: *emotionally distant, high expectations, punishment*

Barb returns to Chelsea's room and sees her playing with LEGOs on the floor of her room.

"What did I ask you to do? Did I ask you to sit and play? No! I stood here five minutes ago and said *very* clearly that you needed to get dressed, go downstairs, eat breakfast, and put your homework in your backpack. You're not the only person in this house who has to be on time this morning, young lady. Now *move it!*"

Possible Response 3: PERMISSIVE

parenting style: *high warmth / low demandingness*

typical qualities: *accepting, lenient, avoiding confrontation*

While sipping coffee and packing Chelsea's lunch, Barb spots Chelsea out of the corner of her eye.

"It's 7:20, kiddo. If we leave soon, you'll be only a little late for school. Here's your lunch. I'm going to finish getting ready myself. You know where the cereal and milk are."

Possible Response 4: UNINVOLVED

parenting style: *low warmth / low demandingness*
typical qualities: *uninterested, competing priorities, passive*

Stu and Barb rush through their own morning routines, eventually meeting near the front door.

Stu: "Where's your daughter?"

Barb: "*My* daughter? It's your morning to take *our* daughter to school."

Stu: "I have to catch my bus. You take her today and I'll do tomorrow."

Barb: "Fine. If she's late, she's late. I'll let her explain it to the front office."

. . . .

Category labels—whether popular or scientific—provide a convenient shorthand. However, these examples show how loving, well-intentioned parents can hop from one style to another, depending on the circumstances. To complicate categorization further, no two parents raising a child together are 100 percent aligned in their styles, just as no single parent is perfectly aligned with the other caregivers in a child's life—grandparents, teachers, coaches, clergy, and so on. Most of the time, parenting feels anything but neatly defined. It can be hard, messy work.

To further complicate matters, parents are just one of many environmental influences on children's cognitive, social, and emotional development. Genes and the interplay between genes and the environment also influence development.[4] If that leaves you feeling like your influence is limited, that's because it is. In fact, the control you have over your child's development is akin to fishing in a river. Although you have control over where you stand, how you cast, and what you put on your hook to tempt the fish, you cannot control the weather, the current, the natural predators, nor where the fish swim.

Of course, raising kids can also be funnier, more enjoyable, and more gratifying than any other activity, including fishing. (Cue the hue and cry from our purist fly-fishing friends.) Those are three of the reasons that grown-ups keep having babies. (Lots of books and movies focus on the other reason.) For maximum benefit to our children and ourselves, our best play is to spend as much time as we can in the Authoritative quadrant.

Some unusual circumstances, such as urgent safety concerns, call for an Authoritarian approach. For example, if your newly licensed teenage driver is about to drift into oncoming traffic because they are reaching for their cell phone, that is a reasonable time to bark an order. And if it happens again, you can revoke their driving and cell phone privileges without warning. In other unusual circumstances, you might be purposely Permissive by indulging your kids. If everyone has had a long day and no one feels like cooking dinner, it could be glorious for your whole clan to curl up on the couch with bowls of ice cream and watch a superhero movie.

What makes these occasional instances of Authoritarian and Permissive parenting work is that they are (1) used sparingly and (2) a good fit to the situation. When used sparingly and fittingly, these departures from Authoritative parenting make sense to our children. Even without the many outcome studies supporting the supremacy of Authoritative parenting, it makes intuitive sense that spending too much time being an Authoritarian or Permissive parent has predictably negative consequences. It also makes sense that no matter how sad, tired, or busy we feel, it is best to spend very little time in the Uninvolved quadrant. Parents who feel themselves drifting into this quadrant regularly should reach out to a friend, relative, clergy, or mental health professional for support, if they can. Uninvolved is rarely any parent's dominant style, but it happens in cases where someone never wanted a child in the first place; or is dealing with a chronic and debilitating medical or mental health problem, such as drug addiction; or is preoccupied by trying to cope with an overwhelmingly adverse set of life circumstances.

A CLOSER LOOK AT AUTHORITATIVE PARENTING

How does Authoritative parenting actually feel, especially in a stressful situation? Parenting is a raggedy challenge, so checking out another realistic example is a valuable way to conclude this chapter. Anyone can commit to the *idea* of being an Authoritative parent, but *being* one takes practice. Consider this parent-child dialogue in which the parent is doing their best to be mindful of their internal, emotional responses to their child and to parent in a way that balances limit setting and high standards with granting their child age-appropriate autonomy.

Amy:	I'm headed out.
Parent:	Out where?
Amy:	I don't know yet. I got a text from Sam, and I guess people are hanging out at the mall.
Parent:	People I know?
Amy:	Probably. I don't know. I didn't exactly ask Sam for a list.
Parent:	OK. But the mall closes in an hour.
Amy:	So?
Parent:	So, I'd like to know what your plans are after the mall.
Amy:	Why do you have to know every detail about my life?
Parent:	I don't. I'm sure there's lots I don't know, as a matter of fact. But I think it's reasonable to ask and for you to tell me where you're going to be. I didn't say you couldn't go, but I'm starting to wish I had.
Amy:	But I don't know . . . not exactly.
Parent:	And what homework do you have for Monday?
Amy:	Really? Are we going to have this conversation?
Parent:	(waits silently, with a neutral facial expression)

Amy: I have French and physics. I've done my French, and physics never takes long . . . maybe an hour. It's fine.

Parent: And oboe practice?

Amy: I practiced this afternoon. You heard me.

Parent: I did. It sounded good. And with everything else we have planned for tomorrow, I'm wondering whether you'll be able to put in a solid practice tomorrow *and* get your physics done? Remember that Uncle Roger and Aunt Yvonne are coming over for brunch tomorrow.

Amy: I can get up early and practice before they get here, and then I can do physics in the afternoon.

Parent: So your normal curfew on Saturday night is 11:00. If you're in bed by 11:30, will you get enough sleep?

Amy: You worry about everything! I can manage my own life, you know.

Parent: Yes, you usually make good decisions. So talk me through it. I'd like to hear your plans for tonight and tomorrow.

Amy: (sighing) All right. I'll be with my friends at the mall for about an hour, I guess, until they close. Then we'll probably go somewhere to eat or over to someone's house, just to hang. I'll text you the plan when the mall closes. And then I guess I'll be home by about 10:30, so I'm not exhausted when I get up tomorrow morning around 8:00-ish.

Parent: OK. That sounds reasonable. And if you're out with your friends and some of them start—

Amy: I know, I know. If there's alcohol or drugs or whatever, I'll just come home.

Parent: OK. Have a good time. See you at about 10:30 tonight.

In this interaction, the parent was quite skillful at collaborating *and* holding firm to reasonably high expectations at the same time. It was a reciprocal interaction where the parent provided a rationale, let Amy reason through some concerns, and shared some decision-making power with her. Obviously, the parent did not ignore Amy when she started heading out (which would have been Uninvolved); nor was the parent's reaction "OK, see you whenever" (which would have been Permissive); nor was it "There's no way you're going out with people I don't know" (which would have been Authoritarian). Instead, the parent was responsive to Amy's wish to hang out with her friends but also assertive about the clear standard of the 11:00 p.m. curfew and the high expectation that homework and instrument practice take priority over recreational time. The parent was flexible about the schedule but still walked Amy through the other demands in her schedule.

Not every parent-child interaction ends in a mature, spontaneous compromise (wouldn't *that* be great?!), but the Authoritative style is most likely to succeed—not just in the moment but also over the long haul. If you can consistently use an Authoritative style, then your child will, over time, internalize your voice of reason and develop the ability to reflect and make mature decisions on their own. That is the ultimate goal, after all. Kids make all kinds of decisions when their parents are not present, and the frequency only increases as they get older. The Authoritative style helps ensure that wisdom keeps pace with independence. By contrast, if parents adopt an Authoritarian style or add excessive, unhealthy pressure to any parenting style, then the outcomes on mental health and behavior can be devastating. Children internalize that controlling, emotionally distant voice and begin talking to themselves harshly. As a result, their sense of self-worth will take a big hit and their mood will plunge each time they fail to meet their parents' unrealistic expectations.

In this chapter, we have tried to do three things: (1) give you a way to categorize your parenting style that is more reliable and valid than pop-culture memes; (2) illustrate how real-world parenting is fluid, not categorical; and (3) emphasize that the Authoritative style—one that is warm, flexible, and responsive *and* sets high expectations, enforces clear rules, and invites discussion about decisions—is associated with the best social, emotional, and academic outcomes. With this framework as a foundation, we can now circle back to the topic of expectations and explore what works and what backfires. Both the Authoritative and the Authoritarian styles place high demands on children, but a hallmark of the Author*itative* style is warmth, a topic so important that it gets its own chapters later in the book.

chapter seven

TAME YOUR CORE EXPECTATION

How to Pivot from Competitive Best
to Personal Best

• TRANSFORMATION 2 •

THE FIRST TIME A STUDENT TOLD ME, "IF I DON'T GET ALL AS AND
A-minuses, my parents will pull me out of school," I assumed it was
teenage hyperbole. The second time, I felt surprised that more than one
set of parents in the world had used such a threat to coax high grades. The
third time, I became a believer because the words came directly out of a
parent's mouth. Sitting right there in my office. I witnessed the Instinct
to Protect pass through the lenses of Culture & Tradition, Family History,
and Individual Identity, refract through the prism of Temperament &
Personality, and land right in front of me. Mr. Larson was unflinching in
his expression of harmful Verbal Pressure, focusing it like a laser beam on
the single outcome of course grades.

"Our expectations are clear, Dr. Thurber," he began, first looking at
his wife and then at me. "If Patrice doesn't get As, then our investment in
her education will have been for naught. We'll simply pull her out and

nroll her in our public school back home—which isn't half-bad, by the way—and she can get As there. You and I both know that there will be less competition at home than here. And while a diploma from this place is nothing to sneeze at," he said, gesturing vaguely toward the window that looked onto campus, "grades matter. There's no denying that."

He was right, of course. Grades do matter. But they do not matter more than mental health. And as the research summarized in earlier chapters makes clear, high levels of anxiety or depression hurt performance. The Pressure Paradox was right there in the room, waiting for a response. "I'm not sure how to weigh the value of a B at this school versus an A at another school," I confessed, "but a focus on Patrice's effort will help her academic performance much more than a focus on grades will, no matter where she is."

Mr. Larson bristled, then answered, "Effort has always been part of the picture—Patrice knows that—but she has to understand how important it is to get high marks. You understand that none of this will have been worth it if she doesn't get into a top university."

PROCESS VS. PRODUCT

Given how competitive admissions are at some colleges and universities, it is understandable that many parents reason as Mr. Larson does.[1] However, the days of a prestigious secondary school serving as a pipeline to a top university disappeared almost a century ago. Therefore, focusing parental expectations on effort rather than outcome, on the *process of learning* rather than the *product of learning*, is the smart choice for both children's mental health and their education. This is the core of **Transformation 2**, but pitching it to Mr. Larson was not easy. Nevertheless, I did convince him to take the threat of school transfer off the table, mostly by offering a vivid description of how much anxiety it had generated in his daughter.

In subsequent sessions with Patrice, I was able to shift her mindset slightly away from As and her overbearing parents. Together, we tried to understand her parents' intent, which was grounded in genuine care and concern. We also discussed how blaming her "idiot" teachers, her "obsessed" parents, and the "boring" content of her classes allowed her to shirk responsibility. Once she stopped finding external causes for her underperformance, Patrice started to notice and appreciate the inherent joy of learning, at least in some of her classes. Ultimately, this mindset shift had positive results for both her mood and her grades. Patrice's parents continued to communicate their high expectations, but they, too, shifted. Besides removing the threat of withdrawal from the school she loved, they tried hard to encourage her efforts—her *personal* best—rather than force her to achieve an absolute, *competitive* best.

THE BENEFITS OF PARENTAL EXPECTATIONS

There is great value and evolutionary utility in parents' communicating expectations to their children. The key lies in what those expectations are and how parents convey them. Expectations can be beneficial for children when they do the following:

- **Maintain Momentum.** Parental expectations are a psychological force that pushes young people along a particular path in life. Parents who state their expectations—for their child's or teen's effort, behavior, decision-making, relationships, and so on—are providing worthy goals and potent motivation. This could be, for example: "My parents expect me to get a summer job instead of just hanging out," or "My parents expect me to treat others with respect, despite the differences between us," or "My parent expects me to put off trying alcohol until after I've graduated from high school."

- **Provide Focus.** Whether the focus is on athletic, artistic, academic, or social-emotional efforts, parental expectations guide children about where to concentrate their time and energy. Most parents have, at some point, helped their child make a choice about what sport to play, what instrument to practice, what book to read, or what friendships to cultivate. Our life experience puts us in a good position to provide coaching of this sort. Most parents also expect these choices to be thoughtful, while allowing for some trial and error. For example, "You've already sustained one concussion, so I'm concerned about another one in either soccer or football. Nevertheless, you can't just sit on the couch. How about running cross-country, at least for one season?"

- **Transmit Generational Knowledge.** In addition to guidance on where to focus a child's energy, parental expectations also transmit the collective wisdom of multiple generations. All parents have culled wisdom, adopted values, and learned lessons from their own parents and grandparents. When our expectations are realistic and positive, they are especially powerful because they are achievable and attractive to our kids. For example, a parent might say, "I understand that your ceramics teacher is not your favorite. Right now, he's having you spend most of your time throwing pots, and you'd like to try some free-form sculpture. It seems to me like both of these skill sets are fundamental to your learning this craft. I've generally had a good experience talking face-to-face with my various coaches and teachers over the years. How about we rehearse what you might say to him after class this week?"

Having distinguished between unhealthy and healthy expectations, as well as having offered a few examples, let us offer a definition: **Parental expectations** are conscious or unconscious hopes or beliefs that caregivers have about how a child will think, feel, and behave. These expectations have the power to bring a child's thoughts, feelings, and behaviors in line with those hopes and beliefs when they are realistic and positive. However, when parental expectations are unrealistic and/or negative, they induce harmful thoughts, feelings, and behaviors. The natural question is then: How can parents avoid expressing unhealthy expectations? The answer is: Emphasize consistent *effort* over specific *outcomes*. In addition, it behooves your child and you to do the following:

- **Check Yourself.** All parents communicate some expectations to their children without realizing that they are doing so. For example, parents who ask their teenage sons, "So, do you have a girl-friend?" may be surprised to learn, a couple of years later, that their gay or bisexual son lived in fear of being disowned because his parents had clearly stated their expectation that he be straight. The implicit heteronormativity of that question may have been outside those parents' awareness. An inclusive question such as, "Any romance in your life?" is less likely to generate fear about conforming, although "What are the most important relationships in your life right now?" is even less likely to convey expectations about having any romantic attachments in the first place. It is indeed challenging, but parents benefit from checking whether their unconscious expectations have leaked into verbal interactions with their child.

- **Ask Your Child.** It sounds simple, but there is no substitute for directly asking your child, "What expectations do you think I have for you?" and "Are any of my expectations—whether I've said them out loud or given you the impression in some other way—bothering you?" You may get only a quizzical look, but you will have made it clear that talking about your expectations is not taboo. You may have to ask again in a month or two, but most children eventually do share their thoughts on the disconnect between what a parent expects and what the child believes is achievable. Listen carefully, even if you disagree, so that you and your child can come to a shared understanding of what you expect and how you can support your child's efforts to learn, mature, and achieve great things.

- **Stay Child-Focused.** All parents live vicariously through their children, to some extent. Just be certain that you customize your expectations for your child to *their* interests, abilities, and personality, not yours. Disaster is just around the corner if you coerce your child to achieve something you wish you had achieved but never did. The emotional side effects of coercing your child in this way are never worth the vicarious sense of success or completion you might feel, nor the temporary bragging rights you might get. Remember, your definition of success will always differ from your child's. Members of the family may share common values, but there are always some differences. Character strengths and specific talents also differ from parent to child. Your strengths may lie in academics, whereas your child's may lie in athletics. Or perhaps you love reading Shakespeare and writing sonnets, but your child prefers watching anime and writing fan fiction. Who knows? Naturally, your values, interests, abilities, and personality will influence your child's. The key is not to graft your passions wholesale onto your child's daily schedule, expecting them to meet or exceed the goals you or your parents set for you back in the day. (If you want confirmation that your child does not want to be you—no matter how much they love you—show them a photo of you from seventh grade and watch their reaction. We promise it will jolt you out of your mini-me reverie.)

- **Appreciate Before You Evaluate.** Beginning at birth, parents evaluate children's behavior as good or bad, often without considering how natural it is or without acknowledging the creativity, determination, or emotion that underlies the behavior. Even cooing to your newborn, "Uh-oh . . . Were we a bad boy? Did we poop again before Daddy had a chance to put on a fresh diaper?" can lead to "Uh-oh . . . How did you do so badly in Spanish this term?" Notice the difference between those questions and these versions: "Uh-oh, did we poop? I guess I need to be quicker next time!" and "Spanish was more of a struggle this term than it was last term." None of this is meant to imply that you should not eventually potty-train your toddler or help improve your middle-schooler's foreign language study skills. Instead, it is a reminder to put all undesirable behavior in a developmental context (by asking, "Is this normal for a kid this age?") and learn more about the upstream *causes* of a behavior before you label its downstream *results*.

One of the reasons Pressure Parents are more likely to cheat on behalf of their children, as with Operation Varsity Blues, is because their expectations are for a competitive best, not a personal best. Support Parents also have high expectations, but they want their children to do *their* best, not *the* best. It does feel amazing when your child's perseverance and effort earn them first place or gain them a coveted spot, but your core expectations should always be about your child's personal best. When kids internalize the parental expectation to do or be their personal best, they become self-motivated, regardless of whether performance on the task yields an external reward (such as an acceptance letter to a particular school), an intrinsic reward (such as the feeling of gratification that comes from tutoring a classmate), or both. Moreover, kids whose parents have high expectations of worthy, personal bests usually do not develop perfectionistic personalities[2] or suffer from anxiety and depression. Instead, they pursue excellence through perseverance and effort.

In sum, Authoritative parenting that emphasizes personal bests is more motivating and yields better performance, compared to a Pressure

Parent's focus on competitive bests. In her research conducted for the National Center for School Mental Health, Orly Termeie and her colleagues concluded that the highest-functioning children had parents who encouraged hard work in school, without being overbearing, and who set high expectations for homework and behavior, but still permitted breaks and learning from mistakes. Students who have this type of balance in their lives, Termeie and her colleagues concluded, also have fewer symptoms of depression.[3]

OVERCOMING YOUR INHERITANCE

If the research is so clear, why do so many parents stumble into the unhealthy Pressure Parent zone? Part of the answer lies in those parents not knowing what the research findings are. (Fortunately, you are now one of those parents who do understand harmful versus healthy pressure.) Another part of the answer lies in how some parents' own parents pressured them. (Not a terribly earth-shattering insight, yet true.) To our roles as parents, we all bring both our unique styles and the legacy of our own parents. Sometimes, the experience of our parents' spoken and unspoken expectations leaks into our parenting. Fortunately, heightened self-awareness helps us shed some of the unhealthy attitudes and behaviors that we inherited from whoever raised us. It also helps us preserve most of the healthy stuff we inherited.

Reflect for a moment to assess whether any current tension between your child and you resembles the tension you had—or perhaps still have—with one of your parents. Consider the case example of Kellen:

KELLEN WAS IN THIRD GRADE WHEN HE LIED TO HIS CLASS about having seen a meteor shower the night before. After a class trip to the local planetarium, Kellen had begged his parents to wake him up at 2:30 a.m., the time the planetary scientist had announced that the meteor shower would start. Kellen's parents had refused, citing the late hour and the importance of sleep.

Earlier in elementary school, Kellen's parents had pressured him to get straight As, describing anything less as "carelessness." Wanting to please his parents (and show he *did* care), Kellen started cheating in small ways, such as writing quiz answers on his palm. His loose relationship with the truth made it easy for Kellen to let his desire to be admired by adults get the best of him.

The day after the field trip, Kellen's teacher and classmates were impressed to hear that he had watched the meteor shower in the middle of the night. For added realism and believability, Kellen added a few details about the timing and direction of the meteors he saw. A week later, Kellen's parents had a parent-teacher conference. When the teacher complimented Kellen's parents on their tireless dedication to their son's science education, his lie was exposed.

Today, the shame of the confrontation with his parents, coupled with his having to apologize to his third-grade class for lying, makes Kellen exquisitely sensitive to his own child's relationship with the truth. When he discovered that his own daughter, Melissa, had lied to her softball coach about having practiced with a teammate over the weekend, Kellen made her apologize to the team for lying, and he forbade her from playing in the next four games.

. . . .

Unhealthy pressure was just one part of the complex relationship between Kellen and his parents. Certainly, additional factors played into Kellen's dishonest behavior as a child, just as they currently play into his own child's dishonesty. As you reflect on how you exert pressure, you may spot previously unnoticed historical factors at play in your current relationship with your child. Kellen's case reminds us to consider the context and plausible origins of parental pressure.

Whereas some Pressure Parents repeat the historical missteps of the previous generation, other Pressure Parents have contemporary psychological wounds that contaminate the parent-child relationship. A few years ago, I worked with one senior, Mina, whose mother was relentlessly critical and overcontrolling. During school vacations—including the summer—Mina's mother insisted that she remain inside their small downtown apartment to study for standardized tests. During more than two years of these restrictions, Mina endured her mother's insistence that her toil would ultimately lead to admission to Harvard, Yale, Princeton, or Stanford. As you might expect, when Mina first came to see me, she was lonely, anxious, and totally opposed to attending one of those schools, "or my mother will feel like she's won, in which case, she'll torture my little brother in the exact same way."

In our second or third meeting, I learned that Mina's father had left the family years ago to pursue his business career and his romance with another woman, thus leaving the mother alone and jobless, in a big city, with the responsibility of raising two children. I am certain that a huge part of this mother's Pressure Parent persona was the result of the abandonment and betrayal at the hands of her husband. The employment challenges posed by her immigrant status probably amplified her ardent desire for her two children to be successful, which she mistakenly but understandably equated with admission to four famous universities.

Other factors were undoubtedly at play in this family system, but I found myself wishing that this mother had the benefit of psychotherapy, as her daughter did. It is plausible that the harmful pressure and severe restrictions she imposed on Mina were her form of coping with the traumatic abandonment she had suffered. Perhaps her behavior was an overcontrolling and displaced expression of anger toward Mina's father. It is hard to know for sure, but psychodynamic insights such as these often help people understand maladaptive behaviors and shift their mindsets. Perhaps some form of supportive individual or family therapy would have allowed Mina's mother to recast her rigid expectations of a *competitive* best into a more flexible set of expectations centered on encouraging

Mina's *personal* best. Adopting personal, flexible expectations might have also helped this parent see the developmental benefit of age-appropriate freedoms and the intellectual benefits of downtime. Mina's case reminds us to withhold judgment—of ourselves and others—in favor of gathering information and garnering support. Unhealthy behavior is almost always a symptom of pain, not malice.

VIRTUAL EXPECTATIONS

Unhealthy pressure also comes from young people's peers, either in face-to-face interactions or via text messages, social media, and dating apps. On popular platforms such as Instagram, users create a highly curated version of their physical selves, as well as their adventures, creations, and social connections. For most users, their online profile is a peacock-like display of outcomes. Precious few posts are about effort, let alone learning from failure. Sure, young people post "fails" on YouTube, as their parents do on Pinterest, but the goal is to be ironic, be humorous, and go viral, not to be honest about how one is beset with a serious struggle. For many adolescents and young adults, the net result (pun intended) of digesting a constant stream of other people's awesome outcomes is to feel depressed about their own seemingly unremarkable life, anxious that they are missing tons of fun gatherings and memorable moments, and pressured to achieve something worthy of a post. Social media fans the flames of kids' competitive selves.

· ·

NIK WAS TWELVE YEARS OLD BEFORE A TEACHER REPRImanded him for the first time. Normally, Nik was well-behaved and respectful of his classmates and teachers alike. However, on the first day of seventh grade, his homeroom teacher, Ms. Fandriski, had asked each student to describe a highlight of their summer. Nik's reply had been, "My summer pretty much sucked."

Mildly concerned about Nik's use of the word *sucked*, Ms. Fandriski had replied, "Excuse me, Nik. What did you say?" Not understanding his offense, Nik used the word again, this time elaborating, "I said that my summer pretty much sucked. Nothing grammable."

"Nothing *grammable*?"

"Nothing for the 'gram, Ms. Fandriski. Nothing worth posting on Instagram," Nik explained.

. . . .

Dating apps, such as Tinder, Bumble, OKCupid, and Grindr, can be more destructive to self-image than other social media apps. The slightly older user demographic is somewhat better at coping with peer pressure, but *hookups* (quick sexual encounters, expressly devoid of emotional investment) put more on the line, and rejections can be especially harsh.

. . . .

TRACY HAD TURNED EIGHTEEN ONE WEEK BEFORE HER FIRST appointment. When I asked her what had brought her in and how I could be helpful, she surprised me with, "You can help me figure out a way to permanently delete dating apps from my phone. I need someone to block me from reinstalling them, 'cause I keep doing that."

"You're conflicted," I said.

"No, I'm certain that I don't want them on there. If they're on there, I waste time, but I would waste time doing something else if they weren't, so that's not what I'm worried about," Tracy explained.

"You know you don't want these apps on your phone, but you have them anyway," I said. "You sound almost addicted, not conflicted."

Tracy was quiet for a few seconds and then said, "Shit. I never thought about it as an addiction, but I think you're right."

"So, what are the good parts about some of these apps?" I asked.

"Well, it feels good when people contact me, you know, and want to talk or meet. And it gets me off campus, so there's a little variety to my social life. The longer I'm here, the smaller this school seems."

"And what are the not-so-good things about being on these apps?" I asked.

"Well, that's why I'm here," Tracy explained. "I end up feeling like shit when I get dumped. I mean, not right away. If things progress from talking to actually meeting, then we usually hook up. That part's fun, but then it's like the other person is all 'See ya later' and stuff and they never want to hook up again."

"Sounds like you want a relationship, not a hookup," I ventured.

"What!? No way, Dr. Thurber. Did you say 'relationship'? God, no. Nobody has time for a relationship." Tracy sat back and looked at me, brow furrowed.

"I definitely missed the mark there," I said. "So it's not about having a relationship, but you would like to see the same person more than once."

"No, it's not even that. I'm a little embarrassed to say, but what the hell. It's just that both the girls and the guys I've hooked up with usually have something to say about my body, and it's made me really self-conscious about my weight, my hair, my breasts . . . everything. One day, someone will say, 'Oh, you have a great . . . you know . . . body,' or whatever, so I feel OK about myself. Then the next week, somebody else will be like, 'Why do you shave your pits, girl? I like it natural.' I come back to campus feeling horrible about my body."

"That's when you delete the apps," I guessed aloud. "At least temporarily."

"No. Before. I'm like not even dressed and I've already deleted the app. I'm like, 'Screw you,' but what I really mean is, 'Screw *me*!' Why do I keep doing this? Why do I care? I don't know, but I do. So, yeah, I delete the apps."

"But then you reinstall them," I said.

"Maybe I should be a psychologist," Tracy joked back. "It seems like fun. Plus, you probably don't care what people think about you." I flashed a *yeah right* smile, and we both laughed.

. . . .

Notice how different the modern forms of peer pressure are from what most parents and grandparents experienced. Most twenty-first-century kids are not pressuring other kids—face-to-face—to take unhealthy risks like smoking a joint behind the dumpster or chugging a beer in the basement. Our impression, in talking with thousands of adolescents, is that the brand of "Doesn't-your-mommy-let-you?" or "What's-wrong?-Are-you-worried-you'll-get-caught?" peer pressure is nearly extinct. Modern peer pressure is insidious, constant, and reflects the actions of both total strangers and a multitude of friends, not two or three. Thanks to carefully curated online profiles, middle school students have the impression that "everyone" is vaping or traveling or having sex or drinking or winning or acting just plain witty. And thanks to dating apps that make no-commitment sexual intimacy normative, many high school and college students have their self-esteem elevated and shattered on a regular basis. Together with pornography (also easily accessible on any smartphone), dating apps have made young people incredibly self-conscious about their height, weight, skin, hair, jawline, cheekbones, breast size, penis size, muscle size, and grooming preferences. The self-consciousness is not new. But it is extreme, and psychologically risky, in new ways.

The pressure to meet or exceed perceived social standards also distorts young people's perception of personal worth—for themselves and for others. (More on this point in Chapter 14.) I once asked an eighteen-year-old senior student about any perceived risks of having brief, sexual relationships with people he found on dating apps. His reply: "Well, I always cross-check them on Instagram. If they have, like, thousands of followers, then I know they're legit." When the number of followers, subscribers, or cyber friends legitimizes a person's character and sanitizes their sexual history, young people have crossed into a virtual world of high vulnerability and dangerously unpredictable pressure.

As parents, we cannot compete with the seductiveness of the internet, but we can provide a healthy counterbalance by sitting with our children sometimes while they interact virtually with their friends, just as we sit with them sometimes when they interact face-to-face with their friends. Older teens will rebuff this overture, of course, but if we start occasionally keeping our kids company when we initially grant them internet access, then they will accept our presence. And our parental presence—more so than anything else—gives us the power to temper some of the most harmful pressures on the internet. Indeed, our children benefit from our presence, our questions, and our observations—about both the virtual and the real world—despite their protests to the contrary. Consider how depressurizing a conversation like the following can be:

Parent: (sitting down next to child) What app are you on?

Byron: (eyes fixed on smartphone) What? None. I was looking at what my teacher posted for homework.

Parent: How does it look?

Byron: What?

Parent: The homework for tonight. How does it look? Doable?

Byron: It's not posted yet. So I'm looking at Instagram.

Parent: (resisting the temptation to focus on Byron's initial deception) Oh. What's happening on Instagram?

Byron: (looking up for the first time) Nothing.

Parent: (resisting the temptation to take Byron's comment literally) What's the most interesting post you've seen today?

Byron: There isn't one.

Parent: But you're double-tapping every photo.

Byron: 'Cause these are my friends.

Parent: So, you're kind of saying "hi" to them.

Byron: Basically.

Parent: Do they say "hi" back?

Byron: (smiling slightly) That's not how Instagram works.

Parent: So show me how it works.

Byron: Why, so you can stalk me on Instagram?

Parent: I'm just interested in what you post.

Byron: For real?

Parent: Well, I'm not sure, because I don't know yet what you post.

Byron: (smiling slightly) Maybe we should keep it that way.

Parent: (resisting the temptation to chastise Byron for his disrespectful comment) I'm just curious. It seems like . . . I mean . . . you spend time on Instagram, so it must be kind of important to you.

Byron: (sighing) OK. Well, today I posted this picture of my french fries. Fascinating, right?

Parent: There must have been something interesting about them.

Byron: I wanted to warn my friends not to eat the fries in the cafeteria because they were so soggy. So I added the caption "limp" and turned it into a meme. Kinda.

Parent: You were looking out for your friends.

Byron: Kinda. But not everyone who follows me on Instagram is a friend.

Parent: Some aren't?

Byron: Well, not Julia Szosdak, for example.

Parent: Because . . . ?

Byron: All she does is post her latest chem grades. Like, "OMG. 95. Why would Mr. Charbonneau take off 5 pts for no units?"

Parent: You feel like she's bragging.

Byron: I'd be psyched with a 95. You know I'm not a STEM guy.

Parent: You judge yourself compared to Julia.

Byron: No. She's an idiot.

Parent: An idiot who gets 95s on chem exams?

Byron: Exactly.

Parent: And an idiot whose posts have made you decide that you're "not a STEM guy"? I didn't realize you let your classmates make those decisions for you.

Byron: They don't. But I'm not getting 95s, that's for sure.

Parent: (deciding to focus on the effects of social media, rather than give a predictable lecture about spending more time studying and less time on Instagram) Would you feel more motivated if you didn't know Julia's exam scores?

Byron: I don't know.

Parent: But you might think about yourself differently?

Byron: I don't know.

Helping your child pivot from their *competitive best* to their *personal best* is gradual and uneven, so we cannot immediately see whether this parent is making headway. In your own parenting, take advantage of any moments of traction you detect. Work to rebuild the motivation that social media and dating apps routinely sap with their relentless talent showcase and critique of beauty, exploits, and achievement. If you do not detect any traction, know that you are still nurturing the parent-child relationship. That good work has its own wonderful benefits. In the example above, the parent's questions and comments do little to change Byron's expectations or dial down the levels of harmful peer pressure. But at least the parent showed some warmth, an essential relationship ingredient we first explored in Chapter 6. That warmth, combined with realistic expectations and a focus on the child's interests (not the parent's), is also a key component of healthy pressure, as we shall see in the next chapter.

chapter eight

INCREASE YOUR WARMTH

How to Convert Nonverbal Pressure
into Tender Emotional Expression

• TRANSFORMATION 3 •

YOU WERE BORN NAKED AND SOAKING WET, WHICH, AS PARENTS ARE fond of reminding children, is a recipe for "catching your death of cold." To lessen that risk, caregivers instinctively dry and swaddle newborn babies. Most other mammal parents behave the same way, instinctively warming newborns, even before feeding them.[1] However, it is not only temperature warmth that parents give newborns when they wipe them off and hold them close. Parents are also imparting interpersonal warmth. Cuddling an infant shelters it from the cold; it also communicates the most powerful message any human ever gets from a parent: *Welcome to the world! I am here for you. I will protect you. I love you for who you are, simply because you are my child.* Parental warmth is therefore a combination of **accepting** the child for who they are, **expressing** love for the child through appropriate touch, self-sacrifice, and talk, and **attending** to the child's needs with compassion.

If this makes intuitive sense to you, consider yourself a modern, enlightened parent. People have not always understood how parental warmth contributes to children's healthy development. As recently as the early twentieth century, psychoanalytic[2] thinkers, such as Sigmund Freud and his daughter Anna Freud, along with behaviorists,[3] such as John B. Watson and B. Fred Skinner, hypothesized that the parent-child bond depended primarily on the gratification of primary drives, such as hunger. These researchers believed that babies and toddlers *depended* on their parents for food and protection, but did not *love* their parents in an affectionate, emotional way. This idea's focus on gratifying biological drives, such as hunger, earned it the nickname the "Cupboard Love" theory of parent-child attachment. Some of this theory's proponents, such as Watson, advocated what we now call Authoritarian parenting, with strict rule enforcement, highly structured environments, emotionally and physically distant interactions, high expectations, and harsh punishments for misbehavior.

Fortunately, for the mental health and overall well-being of our species, scientific studies published in 1958 advanced our understanding about the importance of parental warmth. One batch of data came from the primate laboratory of Harry Harlow, a psychology professor at the University of Wisconsin–Madison. Along with his wife, Margaret Kuenne Harlow, and their colleague Stephen Suomi, Harlow shared data on how much time infant rhesus macaque monkeys spent clinging to two kinds of artificial (or "surrogate") mothers. Like many Victorian-era children, these baby monkeys had been reared in nurseries without much physical or emotional contact with parents. Inside their enclosures, however, the monkeys had a choice of two artificial mother replicas. Neither replica looked much like a monkey, but their inclined, rounded shape, and mother monkey size made them easy for the baby macaques to grab.

What Harlow and his colleagues discovered was that all babies spent much more time clinging to the mother monkey model covered in terry cloth than to the model made of wire mesh. Even when the wire "mother" provided food (in the form of a bottle of milk positioned about where the mother macaque's breasts would be), the babies climbed on that model only to feed. And when the researchers put something frightening in the cage, such as a noisy, marching, wind-up robot, the baby monkeys would always cling to the cloth "mother." Harlow's team interpreted their data as evidence that *comfort and warmth*, not food, formed the core of parent-child attachment.

At the end of his career, Harlow also conducted studies that showed that although food and water were necessary for survival, infant monkeys raised for a year in isolation, deprived of any parental or peer contact, became psychologically unhealthy and withdrawn. Proper nutrition could keep the young monkeys physically healthy, but they were in social-emotional ruin.[4] Not only would these monkeys curl up and withdraw, they would panic when a socially healthy monkey (one who had been raised with other monkeys) was introduced. Despite extensive criticism for their research methods, the Harlows' work provided empirical support for the idea that warm, reliable, interpersonal contact was essential for healthy primate development.

That same year (1958), John Bowlby, who had trained as both a psychologist and a psychiatrist, published his theory that infants have a universal need to seek closeness with their caregiver(s) whenever they feel worried, afraid, or in pain. In his work studying war orphans for the World Health Organization, Bowlby had observed that, like Harlow's frightened monkeys, human infants initially sought parental warmth, not food, when they felt emotional distress. Bowlby labeled behaviors such as crying, stretching out arms, making eye contact, and clinging to caregivers "attachment behaviors" because they are designed to bring caregivers closer. He reasoned that if a parent is reliably present and typically responds warmly to a child's attachment behaviors, then the child develops what Bowlby called a "secure attachment" to the parent.[5]

However, in sparse and understaffed orphanages, where babies' and toddlers' attachment behaviors rarely got responses, Bowlby documented devastating consequences. As with Harlow's monkeys, human infants who had been raised in social isolation, with plenty of food but almost zero interpersonal warmth, were typically withdrawn, depressed, and socially paralyzed. After weeks of social and emotional neglect, they would eventually stop crying, stop stretching out their arms, and—not surprisingly—behave as if they had given up trying to connect with caregivers. As older children, many were persistently depressed, emotionally impaired, and even sociopathic. For Bowlby and many others, it was tragic to realize how much social-emotional damage a severely deprived environment inflicted on children. Despite being clothed, fed, toileted, and housed, children raised without a loving attachment to one or more primary caregivers failed psychologically. Since 1958, science has supported millennia of Support Parent intuition: Surviving and thriving are two very different things.

Having documented the consequences of social-emotional neglect, Bowlby and his close colleague, psychologist Mary Ainsworth, went on to describe the details of how African and American caregivers' warm and reliable responses to young children's expressions of distress helped to create secure attachments.[6] As you might predict, Ainsworth and Bowlby's cross-cultural studies found that securely attached toddlers—those who believed their parent(s) to be warm and reliable—generally turned out to be happy and confident children and teens.

Ainsworth later categorized toddlers' attachment style using a research protocol called "the Strange Situation." She and her team would observe toddlers' behavior while alone in a room with their mother, what happened when a person unknown to the toddler entered the room, then what happened when the parent left for a few minutes, and finally what happened when the parent returned to the room with the stranger and the toddler. The patterns that Ainsworth observed in toddlers' behavior when their parent left the toddler alone with the stranger, as well as when the parent returned, revealed recognizable differences between securely attached and insecurely attached children.

Specifically, Ainsworth found that, when separated from their mother and left alone with a benevolent stranger for a few minutes, securely attached toddlers would show appropriate sadness, followed by appropriate happiness and attachment behaviors (such as outstretching arms to be held) when she returned. By contrast, various types of insecurely attached toddlers would behave in anxious or indifferent ways when the mother left the room. Then, when she returned, they would act uninterested, ambivalent, or hostile. Ainsworth discovered that these different forms of insecure attachment were the result of parents' routinely having responded in cold, unreliable, or angry ways to their child's expressions of distress.[7]

Using parenting-style lingo, we could say that Authoritarian parenting disrupts parent-child attachment but Authoritative parenting creates secure attachment. And secure attachment is a key ingredient of social-emotional well-being, the foundation of thoughts and behaviors that contribute to lifelong success and happiness. In essence, children who grow up believing that they are worthy of others' love, primarily because of how their parent(s) loved them, have the confidence to explore the world, the strength to get up when the world knocks them down, and the motivation to contribute many of their gifts to the world.

At this point, we know what many readers are thinking. *Thanks, guys. That all sounds brilliant, but you should try being warm and reliable when your kid disobeys or ignores you. It's tough.* The truth is, we know. We *have* tried. A few times, we succeeded; other times, we failed. As we discussed in Chapter 6, parents may try to be Authoritative—with high levels of responsiveness and warmth, as well as high levels of control and demandingness—but all parents drift into the Permissive, Uninvolved, and Authoritarian quadrants from time to time. The key to achieving **Transformation 3** is to be self-aware enough to notice when you are drifting so you can return to a warm, reliable style that also upholds high standards.

Now you might be thinking, *But I do show warmth to my kid. And I'm pretty reliable in how I support them, especially when I can see they need it.*

Why isn't it working? The answer introduces a challenging new wrinkle to the unlikely art of parental pressure: It is not how *you* perceive your degree of warmth, it is how your *child* perceives it. Their perception makes all the difference. Relationships are bidirectional, interpersonal interactions, which means your intent can be quite different from your impact. (Remember the Intention Paradox from Chapter 2? Here it is again.)

The example below illustrates how warm versus cold parenting—as perceived by the child—profoundly affects their thoughts, feelings, and behaviors. As you read this example, keep in mind the definition in the first paragraph of this chapter: Parental warmth is a combination of **accepting** the child for who they are, **expressing** love for the child through appropriate touch, self-sacrifice, and talk, and **attending** to the child's needs with compassion. (Conversely, parental coldness is a combination of **rejection**, **reticence**, and **ignoring**.) Also keep in mind that whether a parent's behavior is warm or cold depends entirely on whether the *child* perceives the parent's behavior as caring or not.

. . . .

BRANDY ASKS HER FATHER, SCOTT, FOR HELP WITH MATH homework one night. He replies, "Of course, but first I have to make a few phone calls for work. Why don't you get started on your English homework and I'll come find you in your room as soon as my calls are done."

Brandy replies, "OK," and returns to her room to complete other assignments. She recognizes her father's usual response of *Yes, but later.*

Three hours later, she has completed everything—including her best attempt at math—brushed her teeth, and fallen asleep. When Scott knocks and gets no reply, he gently opens her bedroom door and sees his daughter sleeping peacefully. He thinks, *I'm glad she figured out her math homework.* He takes heart in knowing that Brandy is self-reliant and that he is a devoted father who fulfilled his promise to come find her in her room after he completed his work calls.

A few nights later, Scott is again completing some work he brought home and Brandy is in her room, chipping away at her homework. Just before shutting his laptop, he opens a new tab to access Brandy's grades from the school's parent portal. He is alarmed to discover a C– mark on the most recent math exam. Laptop in hand, Scott walks down to Brandy's room and opens the door. "What's this?" he asks, rotating the laptop toward her. "You're not a C– student . . . certainly not in math."

Brandy does not look up from her English book. "Since when do you care?" she asks sarcastically.

Stunned, Scott can't speak for a moment. Then he says, "Since forever. Wait. What are you even talking about? You know how much I care about you. And not just your grades, either!" He shouts, "You need to tell me if you're struggling in school! I care about your future, damn it!"

Brandy's voice gets softer, and she continues to stare down at her desk. "Sure, Dad. I can tell how much you care by how you're yelling at me."

. . . .

Scott is shocked by his daughter's criticism because he thinks of himself as a warm parent. When Brandy asked for help with math, he agreed to help her. He definitely remembers having helped her with different homework assignments in the past. In fact, he once gave up the better part of a weekend to help her construct an awesome volcano for her third-grade science class. Pyroclastic flow.

For her part, Brandy frequently perceives her father's style as cold. His words "Of course, but first I have to . . ." are his usual prelude to an unfulfilled promise. Most of the time, his actions suggest that work comes before family. Brandy has come to resent her father's treating her as an afterthought, and like most people, she dislikes being yelled at, especially by a parent. Seen through Brandy's eyes last night, her father had all three indicators of cold parenting: rejection, reticence, and ignoring. He **rejected** Brandy's aptitude when he said, "You're not a C– student . . . certainly not in math," when, in fact, that mark was an accurate reflection of her understanding at the time. He was **reticent**, meaning that he was silent about his own feelings of disappointment, worry, and sadness. (He did express shock and anger, but that is distinct from expressing his true, underlying emotions.) Scott also never asked about Brandy's feelings. Instead of pausing to experience how he felt and then communicate his emotions, he let his anger at himself flip into anger at Brandy. It may have angered Scott even more when Brandy called him out by saying, "Sure, Dad. I can tell how much you care by how you're yelling at me." Finally, according to Brandy's recollection, her father has repeatedly **ignored** her requests for support. True, Scott has helped his daughter in the past. And true, he did say he would help her later that night. But Brandy *feels ignored* when her father overprom-ises and under-delivers.

How does cold parenting (in the eyes of children) contribute to harmful pressure? For the answer, first consider the messages that Scott's verbal and nonverbal behavior are sending:

1. I think of you as an A or B student, not as a C student.
2. I judge you based on outcomes (in this case, grades), not on your effort.
3. I will become angry, not inquisitive, when you underperform or when you criticize me.
4. I will leave you on your own to figure things out most of the time, even after I have promised to help.

If these messages are repeated, if instances of cold parenting become a pattern, then they will transform a medium-pressure, "personal best" scenario into a high-pressure, "do-or-die" scenario. Preparing for a math test will be about more than math; it will be about Brandy trying to pre-serve her sense of self-worth (as a competent student), about avoiding her father's anger, and about preserving her father's love. The result, according to the research: decreased self-esteem, increased anxiety, and higher odds of cheating on the future tests.

A warmer response would have been to say, "I'm happy to help you tonight. I also have a few phone calls to make for work. How about if we work together now for twenty or thirty minutes? After that, you could do a few math problems on your own—or maybe tackle some other homework—while I do my calls. If you finish your other homework before I finish my calls, text me. I'll wrap up any call I'm on so we can either do more math, if you need to, or we can just visit a little before you go to sleep."

As you can see, parenting with warmth does not require dropping your other obligations or becoming your child's servant. (In fact, children benefit from hearing their parents think aloud about managing the multiple demands on their time.) Parenting with warmth does require **accepting** the child for who they are (such as a child who needs extra help with some academic work, despite being intelligent); **expressing** unconditional love for the child through appropriate touch, self-sacrifice, and talk (such as spending time together, regardless of the child's homework progress); and **attending** to the child's needs with compassion (such as tutoring them, even during busy times).

Compared to cold parenting, warm parenting during childhood and adolescence typically predicts better mental health and stabler relationships later in life.[8] Partly, this is because of a phenomenon called *emotional contagion*, which stokes the flames of many parent-child conflicts. Before sharing an example, we want to describe the distinctions among *feelings*, which are the bodily sensations that people experience in response to some stimulus; *emotions*, which are labels for the subjective, blended experience of thoughts and feelings; and *affect*, which is the observable expression of emotion.

Seeing a large spider crawl across the ceiling while you are lying in bed may give you a creepy *feeling* that includes rapid heart rate, prickles on the back of your neck, and a hollow sensation in your stomach. You might label the *emotion* as fear. And your *affect* might include wide eyes, a shaky voice, and a grimace. In emotional contagion, children *feel* (have a bodily reaction to) a parent's *affect* (how the parent expresses their emotions). Regardless of whether anyone has labeled the feeling, children begin to experience the same or a similar feeling.[9]

If your young child were lying next to you when you spotted the spider, you can imagine how differently they would respond if you calmly said, "Check it out . . . up there on the ceiling. That's a bigger spider than I'm used to seeing inside. What kind do you think that is? I should probably get a plastic cup so we can trap it and set it free outside," compared to if you warned, with a quivering voice, "Don't move a muscle. There's a huge spider on the ceiling, and it could be poisonous and drop down on us at any moment. On the count of three, let's each roll off our side of the bed, and I'll call the exterminator."

Imagine a parent happening upon a teenager who is messaging friends instead of completing chores. Now see whether you can detect the cold parenting and the emotional contagion that cause the following interaction to deteriorate:

Mother: (sarcastically) Oh, that's perfect, Nadine. While you're chatting, why don't you give a little online poll to see how many of your friends remembered to take the garbage out at *their* house tonight?

Nadine: Mom, please. I'm kinda in the middle of something. (lifts eyebrows and holds up smartphone)

Mother: My point exactly. Two hours ago, you said you'd take out the kitchen garbage, so I bagged it up and put it by the door. And now the hallway smells like sh—

Nadine: (interrupting) Mom! I'm—

Mother: (raising her voice)—and the dog just busted open the bag, and now there's crap all up and down the hallway!

Nadine: (yelling sarcastically) Could you possibly be a little bit
  more intrusive?!

Mother: (also yelling) Could you be a little bit *less* responsible?!

In this scenario, the mother, who had been in a decent mood, walked down the hallway and had a visceral reaction when she saw and smelled garbage everywhere. She started *feeling* hot and shaky, no doubt amplified by surges of adrenaline and cortisol, two stress hormones. Her racing thoughts of *Damn it! Nadine promised she would take the garbage out!* combined with her feelings to create the *emotion* (subjective experience) of anger. When the mother spots Nadine sitting and texting, her *affect* (expressed emotion) comes out in the form of sarcasm and shouting. In turn, the mother's tone and volume make Nadine begin feeling hot and shaky. Combined with Nadine's thoughts of annoyance (at having been interrupted) and guilt (for having neglected her chores), her hot and shaky feelings transform into the emotion of anger. Nadine's subjective experience of anger may be different from her mother's, but her angry affect—yelling and sarcasm—are a lot like her mother's: belittling and toxic. That is emotional contagion.[10]

Returning to parenting style, you might ask: *Doesn't the parent in this scenario have every right to be angry?* The answer is: Of course! The difference between warm and cold parenting is not in the *emotions* that we feel but in the *affect* we display—how we express our feelings. Our emotional expression shapes our children's perceptions—in this case of warm versus cold parenting. In the example above, the angry mother began her interaction with a sarcastic tone, an insulting question, and a put-down about her daughter's friends. The child's perception of her parent's style is likely to be cold, not warm. The mother was **rejecting**, although she was not **reticent** about her feelings. It is unclear whether she **ignored** a bid for attention, but she did ignore her daughter's social needs. Compare what parenting with warmth might sound like, anger and all:

Mother: (holding up her index finger) Nadine?

Nadine: Mom, please. I'm kinda in the middle of something. (lifts eyebrows and holds up smartphone)

Mother: (smiling wanly; speaking firmly) Thanks, I can see that. I know you want to keep texting, but I need to talk with you. Please mute your line for a second.

Nadine: I'm texting. There is no *mute*. (turning phone over) What is it?

Mother: I'm angry. A couple of hours ago, you said you'd take out the trash, so I bagged it up and you watched me put it by the door.

Nadine: I said I'd take it out and I will, but—

Mother: Well, that's the thing. The garbage can't sit there or it starts to stink up the place. Even worse—this time, the dog has torn open the bag, and there's crap all over the hallway. Can you see now why texting needs to wait?

Nadine: Oh boy.

Mother: (silent . . . waiting)

Nadine: OK. Give me like five minutes to wrap this up, and I'll help you clean up.

Mother: I'll give you one minute, then you need to take care of the mess. Please. And I'm making lunch right now, so this is on you.

Nadine: Fine. I'll clean it up myself.

Mother: Yup. And next time, you will—

Nadine: Yes, yes . . . I know! You don't need to say it.

Mother: OK. Thank you. One minute.

In this version, the parent is feeling just as angry, but she tempers her affect. The way she expresses her emotions prevents too much contagion. She is **accepting**, simply by recognizing that teenagers text their friends, forget responsibilities, and set different priorities from adults. As a parent, she does not have to like that set of circumstances, but she refrains from attacking Nadine for being a normal teenager who wants the freedom to socialize with her friends. The mother **expresses** her unconditional love both by mentioning her own contributions to the family (bagging the garbage, making the lunch), by providing some kindness ("Please") and empathy ("I know you want to keep texting"). She also does a great job not responding in kind to Nadine's wisecrack, "I'm texting. There is no *mute*." Many parents would have lost their patience at this point, taken the bait, and transformed the conversation into an argument laden with sarcasm. Also, despite there being a rather urgent and disgusting situation in the hallway, the mother is **attending** to the child's needs with compassion when she interrupts politely but firmly and when she gives Nadine one minute (not five) to wrap up her texting before cleaning up. At a deeper level, the mother is attending to Nadine's clear need to become more reliable, responsible, and helpful. The mother's silence after Nadine's offer to assist ("I'll help you clean up") was a powerful prompt that allowed Nadine to consider her options, recognize her responsibility, and choose to clean up on her own. This is a classic example of Authoritative parenting—a style that balances warmth (primarily expressed as understanding) with high standards (primarily expressed as consistent expectations of the child's personal best).

You can experiment with different expressions of warmth to see what yields the best results—both in terms of compliant behavior from your child and in terms of the whole family's mental health. And although you can control your own thoughts and behaviors, you cannot control those of your child, which means the wrinkle persists: Parental warmth still hinges on children's perceptions. Fortunately, there is a solution—a way to turn up the heat—that ensures kids feel the warmth we parents intend.

chapter nine

TURN UP THE HEAT

How to Express Warmth That Comes from Your Heart, Not Your Head

• TRANSFORMATION 4 •

WHEN IT COMES TO COMMUNICATING WARMTH, MANY PARENTS
fall into two traps. The first trap is equating warmth with permissiveness—letting children do or have whatever they want. But lowering standards, eliminating responsibilities, and abolishing consequences are not signs of love. The second trap is presuming that warmth is an intellectual exercise, as if memorizing and repeating some stock phrases could transmit warmth. The truth is that parental warmth must be genuine, not generic. You have to *feel* accepting, loving, and caring in your heart before you can express it in a way that your child *perceives* as warmth. You do this already sometimes, perhaps without realizing it. In this chapter, we add four strategies to your emotional toolbox that, when combined, greatly enhance your natural ability to parent with warmth.

We know that it can feel uncomfortable, even threatening, to recognize that some of your well-intentioned parenting may have slowed your child's progress or even made things worse. We also know that if you have gotten this far into the book, then you have the courage to continue, so strap in for the ride. If you want to *feel* the kind of warmth in your heart that your child will *perceive* as such, then your next step toward achieving **Transformation 4** is **introspection**. As parents, we must all learn how to recognize, understand, and express *our* feelings. Only then will we be able to parent with warmth. Here are some concrete strategies to help you do that.

1. HEAR FEELINGS

As parents, we tend to hear the words that come out of our child's mouth more than the feelings behind those words. Imagine you are sitting with your child at dinner, and she says, "None of my friends can f***ing believe that you're the new high school principal." Your reaction would be different, depending on whether your child is seven, seventeen, or twenty-seven. Regardless of age, most parents would immediately respond to the profanity. In an angry or disapproving tone, you might say anything from "Who has taught you to speak like that?" or "Don't you ever use that word in this house!" to "Excuse me?!" or "Hey!" and so on.

By latching on to the uncouth behavior, you would have missed an opportunity to respond to the affect—the expressed emotion—in what your child said. So what *does* a kid feel when their parent becomes the principal? Proud? Surprised? Worried? Embarrassed? Anxious? Pressured? Some combination? You might not know, but you surely have a guess, and that is the best place to start when you are trying to hear someone's feelings.

2. ADOPT AN AFFECTIVE MINDSET

Next, you can adopt what psychologists call an *affective mindset*. This is where you register what the child is saying and how they are behaving, but your goal is to discern what the child is feeling. With an affective mindset, you definitely hear the words "None of my friends can f***ing believe that you're the new school principal," but what you think is something like: *Wow. She usually doesn't swear, so there's probably some intense or unusual emotions bubbling under the surface. And even though she said that her friends can't believe my promotion to principal, now I'm wondering whether she is the one who is most shocked.* Or maybe you think, *Hmm . . . she's commenting about her friends, which reminds me how important those peer connections are. She's probably feeling a lot of anxiety and pressure to have me suddenly in a leadership role that includes discipline. What if I had to require one of her friends to withdraw for plagiarism or something?*

As you can see, there are many plausible guesses about the subtext of someone's stated emotions or underlying feelings. Maybe we should call "adopting an affective mindset" *being an affect detective.* That is really what you are doing—assembling all the clues you have to figure out what the thoughts and feelings are, deep down. And with regard to the profanity, you might think, *I disapprove of the foul language, so I'm going to say something and maybe impose a consequence. But not now. She's too fired up to listen to my opinion on swearing right now.* Those sorts of silent reflections are all part of your new affective mindset, all part of being an affect detective when you hear feelings.

3. EXTINGUISH SPARKS

When your child pushes your buttons, you feel it. Like it or not, all parents have interpersonal sensitivities—tender spots that, when touched, evoke an unusually strong emotional reaction inside us. Some of us seethe when our child is rude or acts entitled. Some of us go nuts when our child ignores us. Some of us have a meltdown when our child forgets a chore we asked them to do. Every parent has different buttons, but all buttons have one thing in common: They are not actually buttons but old psychological wounds.[1] Like the embers of a dwindling campfire that emit an untidy shower of hot sparks when someone throws on a fresh log, old psychological wounds lie dormant until someone perturbs them. One parent described his child this way:

FOR ME, IT'S ALL ABOUT BEING TRUTHFUL. WHEN I CATCH my child lying to me, even about something small, I just lose it. The other day, I asked him whether he had brushed his teeth.

He looked me straight in the eyes and said, "Yeah, Dad," when I knew, 100 percent, that we had run out of toothpaste the day before.

So when I asked him, "What with?" he knew he was busted. At that point, I just couldn't contain myself, and I unloaded with a long, angry lecture about how important it is to tell the truth and how much I hated it when he lied to me.

Later that night, my wife and I were processing what had happened, and she asked about my reaction. I mean, we both think that brushing teeth is important, but the real issue was honesty, not oral hygiene. We agreed on that, too, but when she said that she'd been surprised by how strong my reaction was, I thought more about it.

Honesty is important to every parent, but I know why it's one of my buttons. I remember asking my mother one night—after a particularly nasty argument that she'd had with my dad—whether they would ever get divorced. She promised they wouldn't, but a few years later, they did.

I'm not sure now—as an adult and a parent myself—whether my mother was telling me what she thought I *wanted* to hear or whether she really *believed* that she and my father would stay married, but her forsaken promise left me feeling raw and distrustful for quite a while. Of everyone. Of the world.

Ever since then, I can't stand it when someone lies to me, especially if they're trying to placate or protect me from the truth. I know that's why my son's lying about having brushed his teeth sent me into a tailspin.

· · · · · · · · · · · · · · · ·

Unearthing and understanding an old psychological wound can take more than a single conversation or an evening of self-reflection. Sometimes it takes months of therapy. Fortunately, keeping your cool in the moment—*extinguishing sparks*—does not require knowing exactly what the wound is. As parents, we simply need to recognize an emotional over-reaction when we feel it and try not to go ballistic the next time our kid pushes that button. If your affect is explosive, it eclipses your message. But if you can keep your cool, even while expressing a strong negative emotion, your child is more likely to hear the message.

If we return to the campfire analogy, imagine putting out an errant ember with your shoe to prevent it from igniting something outside the firepit where it landed. If the parent in the teeth-brushing example is able to feel his blood begin to boil the next time his child lies to him, he can extinguish this emotional spark by saying to himself, *I recognize this rush of anger. My kid just hit a nerve, so let me take a second or two before I respond. That way, I'm less likely to overdo it.* We have to emphasize that this "second or two"—this equanimity—is a muscle. You cannot just decide to stay cool next time your kid pushes one of your buttons. It takes time and practice to snuff your emotional sparks.

4. EXPRESS EMPATHY

Empathy is a powerful way to express warmth, calm a feisty temper, share delight or dismay, and—above all—connect with your child. Empathy is also the most misunderstood and underutilized tool in most parents' social-emotional toolbox, so we have included many examples in this section. Whereas *sympathy* is feeling the same sorrow or pity that another person feels because of some hardship, *empathy* is expressing an understanding of whatever positive or negative things another person is feeling or thinking.

In an effort to express empathy, many loving parents will involuntarily trivialize, apologize, sympathize, distract, or problem-solve. Here is what that can sound like:

Empathy FAILS

Parent: What's wrong, Bona?
Bona: Nothing.
Parent: Nothing?
Bona: I just found out that Robin is taking someone else to the dance.
Parent: Relax, hon, there will be other dances.

(*TRIVIALIZING*)

OR

Parent: Gee, I'm sorry that happened.

(*APOLOGIZING OR SYMPATHIZING*)

OR

Parent: Ah, forget Robin. Who needs Robin? Let's watch a movie.

(*DISTRACTING*)

OR

Parent: OK, so let's think of someone else you could go with.

(*PROBLEM-SOLVING*)

After any of the four responses above, most parents would give themselves high marks on empathy without realizing they had failed to provide any.

Here is a nearly foolproof way to nail empathy every time: Before you utter what you *intend* to be empathy, check whether what you are about to say has an adjective that describes a thought or a feeling. There are other ways to express empathy, but mastering this adjective-based method comes first. Here are some examples of what basic empathy can sound like:

Empathy SUCCESSES

> **Parent:** What's wrong, Bona?
> **Bona:** Nothing.
> **Parent:** Nothing?
> **Bona:** I just found out that Robin is taking someone else to the dance.
> **Parent:** Mmm. You must feel pretty disappointed.
> (EMPATHY ADJECTIVE = *DISAPPOINTED*)

OR

> **Parent:** Wow. That's an unwelcome piece of news.
> (EMPATHY ADJECTIVE = *UNWELCOME*)

OR

> **Parent:** With all the positive vibes you got last week, I'm guessing you're pretty confused.
> (EMPATHY ADJECTIVE = *CONFUSED*)

OR

> **Parent:** You probably feel hurt, to say the least.
> (EMPATHY ADJECTIVE = *HURT*)

Immediately, most parents spot two risks with this "nearly foolproof" technique.

- **Risk #1**: The empathic statements above sound canned. With a genuine tone, they are not too bad, but it is true that uttering a stock phrase will earn you an instant eye roll from your kid, so follow the advice we gave in Chapter 3: Talk how you usually talk. Maybe "Boy, that must have felt like crap" sounds better. Be authentic in your language if you want your child to listen.

- **Risk #2**: You might guess incorrectly about how your kid is thinking or what they are feeling. Here, the solution is automatic. If "felt like crap" or "hurt" or any other description is not accurate, your child will usually set you straight. (Comforting thought, right? Even more heartwarming is that most kids are happy to set parents straight even when the parents are right. Bliss.) Even when you miss the mark, you will have achieved your goal of expressing compassion and making an emotional connection.

Here is how "empathy auto-correct" might sound:

Empathy AUTO-CORRECT

> **Parent:** What's wrong?
> **Bona:** Nothing.
> **Parent:** Nothing?
> **Bona:** I just found out that Robin is taking someone else to the dance.
> **Parent:** Yikes! I bet you're shocked.
> (WRONG EMPATHY ADJECTIVE = SHOCKED)
>
> **Bona:** Not really. It's happened before. I'm mad now.
> (CORRECT EMPATHY ADJECTIVE = MAD)
>
> **Parent:** I didn't know this had happened before. Now I get why you're mad.

When you express genuine empathy, you make a powerful connection with your child *without solving the problem* that generated the feeling in the first place. Trying to problem-solve in an emotionally intense moment is generally futile. However, even if you wait for strong feelings to subside on their own, your child is unlikely to collaborate in any problem-solving if they believe you do not grasp their experience. (Or, as kids put it, "You just don't get it!") Empathy is the admission ticket to your child's soul. They will not let you in until they feel understood.

Why, then, is such a potent and simple technique so rarely used? Three reasons: (1) we delay empathy, believing that solving the problem first is the best approach; (2) we skip empathy, believing that it is tantamount to agreement; or (3) we provide quick and cursory empathy, immediately shifting into problem-solving mode.

Here is what that last pitfall—empathy negated by problem-solving—sounds like:

Problem-Solving PITFALL

Bona: I just found out that Robin is taking someone else to the dance.

Parent: You're probably shocked, but you gotta pick yourself up and move on. There are other fish in the sea, ya know. Let's think about who else you could go with. How about Charlie?

Bona: (sarcastically) Oh, brilliant. Thank you. I had no idea there were other people I could go to the dance with. Sorry . . . I'm just . . . and Charlie? *Please.*

Saying "You're probably shocked" was empathic, yet it had a limited effect because the parent added some problem-solving in the very same sentence. For empathy to connect two people, it needs time to sink in.

You may have a dozen stellar ideas for solving a particular problem, but connection—which is what people want far more than solutions when they feel upset—requires you to lead with empathy and then pause. Literally, pause. Give your child time to reflect and respond. Afterward, there will be time for you to help your child solve the problem (if they cannot solve it themselves, which they can most of the time), but only after they feel understood. Until then, you are likely to get a cheeky response like in the example above.

Disagreement is another reason why parents who equate empathy and agreement may choose not to use empathy in the first place. If you feel that your child's distress is unwarranted, why would you bother giving them empathy?

Here are two examples of what it might sound like for a parent to skip empathy because they disagree with the premise or disapprove of the situation:

Disagreement PITFALLS

Bona: I just found out that Robin is taking someone else to the dance.

Parent: Really? Good. Why? What happened? Robin discovered that you actually prefer sports over weed?

OR

Bona: I just found out that Robin is taking someone else to the dance.

Parent: It's just as well, Bona. Robin's an idiot, and those dances are just an excuse for everyone to grind on each other.

In reality, empathy and agreement are two different things. *I understand how you feel* or *I understand what you are thinking* are not at all the same as *I agree with you* or *If I were you, I would feel and think the same thing*. Whether or not you agree with or approve of whatever is causing your child's distress, your primary goal is to connect, to be warm. Communicating disapproval of your child's thoughts and feelings does the opposite. Most children would perceive a response such as "It's just as well" as distant and cold. Adding "Robin's an idiot" deepens the chill because it criticizes not only Robin but also Bona. After all, what does it say about Bona's character if they wanted to go on a date with an idiot?

But Robin is *an idiot*, this parent might be thinking. *I just have to get Bona to see that*. Good. Like other loving parents, this mother or father wants to impart wisdom to their child. But again, empathy *must* come first. If you think your child will benefit from looking at a circumstance differently (from your point of view, for example), then it is even more important to lead with empathy. Why? Imagine that the emotional connection between you and your child is a bascule drawbridge (the kind that splits in the middle as the sections tilt up) and your wisdom is a truck, full of helpful advice. Now imagine that something happens to make your child feel unhappy. Naturally, you will want to help solve the problem that caused the distress. However—and this is key—the emotional event has lifted the two leaves of the drawbridge. They have gone from connected, horizontal sections of bridge to disconnected and nearly vertical. There is a massive gap where there used to be a connected roadway. Your truck of wisdom may be full of good ideas, but if you try to drive it across the bridge now, it will crash against a vertical section of bridge or tumble into the water below. By the same token, if you try to communicate something important to your child while they are upset, the message is likely to crash or tumble.

Because strong emotions cloud thinking, people cannot process complex solutions in moments of significant distress. Once they feel understood, because someone they trust has offered some version of "I get what's going on for you right now," their head will be clear enough to think about possible solutions. So, you see, expressing empathy is not just a hallmark of warm parenting, it is what lowers the drawbridge.

With the emotional connection to your child reestablished, you can drive your truck of wisdom across and ask whether they are interested in any of the contents.

5. LISTEN SILENTLY

What gives empathy its power is the silence that follows, so silent listening gets its own little section here. As we advocated a few pages ago, avoid contaminating a wonderfully empathic statement with a preemptive solution or judgment. Instead, express empathy and then fall silent. Full stop. No more. Just say what you think your kid is feeling, then be quiet and listen. Let your child absorb your empathic statement. Accurate or not, your attempt sends a strong message that you care. Then, let your child respond, no matter how long it takes. Usually, your child will reciprocate your warmth. Even if they sound annoyed, their response acknowledges your attempt. You are lowering the drawbridge.

Here is what an exchange might sound like when the parent remembers to listen silently:

Empathy ABSORPTION

Bona: I just found out that Robin is taking someone else to the dance.

Parent: Really? I bet you feel devastated.

(EMPATHY ADJECTIVE = *DEVASTATED*)

Bona: Devastated? Hardly. Why do you think everything is such a huge deal? I'm totally fine.

Parent: (*silent . . . letting the child absorb the empathic statement, "I bet you feel devastated," even if it was inaccurate . . . swallowing the defensive retort that came to mind . . .*

waiting for a possible revision to the characterization of "devastated" . . . resisting the temptation to problem-solve . . . still waiting)

Bona: It's not like I can't find someone else to go with. I'm just . . . I don't know . . . sick of being disrespected.
(CORRECT EMPATHY ADJECTIVE = SICK [OF BEING DISRESPECTED])

Parent: You're annoyed with how Robin treats you.
(GOLDEN EMPATHY. THE PARENT DEMONSTRATED UNDERSTANDING WITHOUT PARROTING BONA'S WORDS.)

Bona: Hello? That's what I've been trying to say.
Parent: It took me a minute to understand.
(AWESOME EQUANIMITY. THE PARENT IGNORED THE CHILD'S IRRITATED TONE AND STAYED FOCUSED ON EXPRESSING EMPATHY.)

Bona: (sighs heavily) So now what?

The parent in this scenario has achieved five monumental successes in just three casual utterances. First, they responded to Bona's strong affect by expressing empathy. Second, they followed empathy with silence and did not take the bait when criticized. Third, they revised their empathic statement by providing a summary that captured how Bona felt. Fourth, they acknowledged having initially mischaracterized their child's emotion *without apologizing*. And fifth, they resisted, *for a second time*, the temptation to jump in with words of wisdom or a quick fix.

Throughout this brief interaction, Bona's parent stayed focused on building an emotional connection by expressing empathy. Not surprisingly, this parental warmth was soothing, Bona gradually became calmer, and eventually asked for the parent's help ("So now what?").

Not all kids ask for help, but they all hate the help we thrust upon them without first listening and understanding. In fact, even after you have expressed empathy, it is a good idea to ask, "Do you want some help thinking about possible solutions?" Asking permission to assist your child will give them some comforting control over what might have initially felt like a loss of control. They may not have had a say in what upset them, but now they have a say in how to cope and in what their next move is.

Hearing feelings, adopting an affective mindset, extinguishing sparks, expressing empathy, and **listening silently** are five potent ways to increase parental warmth. Each takes practice, each works alone and in combination, and all of them complement one another. Getting better at one technique will increase your skill using the four other techniques. As a bonus, there are additional ways to express warmth to your child, to "turn up the heat," many of which vary across cultures. A glimpse at these different approaches is an inspiring way to conclude this chapter.

WARMTH AROUND THE WORLD

Jennifer Lansford is a developmental psychologist who led an international research team in conducting a ten-year study on the ways parents around the world express love for their children.[2] In Sweden, for example, parents express love by treating children almost as equals, encouraging them to express themselves, and honoring their opinions in making family decisions. By contrast, traditional Chinese parents express love by making many decisions for their children. According to Lansford et al.'s research, Chinese fathers have become increasingly nurturing and affectionate toward children as traditional gender roles have blurred. In Colombia and in many Latinx families in the US, parents express love by placing the family's needs before any individual's needs and by adhering to authority within the family. According to Lansford and her team, Italian parents show love through high levels of involvement and emotional expression. By contrast, Thai parents put a premium on respect and nonaggression, both core tenets of Buddhism, the dominant religion in Thailand. And in the US, with its pioneer legacy, many parents show love by promoting their child's individual interests and giving them freedom to make their own choices. Lansford et al.'s research illuminates some fascinating parenting differences between cultures. In the US and other countries, the researchers also found significant within-culture variety.

Whatever form it takes, parental warmth requires some understanding of both the cultural context and the thoughts and feelings you and your child are experiencing. The introspection and interpersonal interaction required to achieve this understanding might make you feel uncomfortable, even intimidated. Nevertheless, we encourage you to reread the examples in Chapters 8 and 9 to appreciate the various ways parental warmth can extinguish harmful pressure.

With great respect for the cultural variations in parenting style and emotional expression, we believe that every parent can find culturally congruent ways to nurture a warm relationship with their child or children. To support that growth, the next chapter illustrates how to use three types of communication—praise, criticism, and questions—to get your messages across clearly, even emphatically, without increasing harmful pressure.

chapter ten

EARN RESPECT, NOT REBELLION

How to Build Connections by
Cracking Kids' Secret Code

• **TRANSFORMATION 5** •

FOR DECADES, I (CHRIS) HAVE ENJOYED FACILITATING *CRACKING KIDS'*
Secret Code, my favorite communication workshop for parents. We
watch clips from some great films featuring parent-child dialogue, such
as *The Sandlot, This Boy's Life, Traffic,* and *Ordinary People.* Following
each clip, I ask three sets of questions, each set more difficult than the
last: (1) What is something you heard a character say? What dialogue do
you remember? (2) What do you think the character *really meant* when
they said that? In other words, what was the subtext or "secret code" of
their statement? (3) What's one way you could respond with empathy *to
the subtext,* to the underlying meaning? In other words, what is something you could say to help the characters in this scene feel understood?

Most parents—regardless of their age, education, income, ethnicity,
gender identity, and so on—are excellent at the first question set, pretty
good at the second, and terrible at the third.

Here is a memorable example from the movie *Stepmom*. In one scene, the biological mother, Jackie (played by Susan Sarandon), is riding horses with her two children across a sunny meadow. It is one day after the children spent an afternoon with their stepmom, Isabel (played by Julia Roberts), in Central Park. The younger child, a boy named Ben, is talking about his having wandered off and gotten lost in the park. Ben feels remorse and guilt, partly because his mother blames Isabel, the stepmom, for the incident. Although a police officer had eventually found Ben, his mother raged against his stepmother and father in front of both children at the police station. Now, in an attempt to pacify his mother by shifting the blame, Ben says, "Mommy? It's not Isabel's fault I ran away." His mother agrees, remarking, "No, that's your fault." She then returns to blaming Isabel, stating, "But it's her fault for not watching over my precious son, as if it were her priority. Which means, her most important job." Ben tries a few more times to exonerate Isabel, citing some of her positive attributes. Each time, Jackie responds with sarcasm. Eventually, Ben says, "I think she's pretty," to which his mother's smug response is, "Sure . . . if you like big teeth." Ben thinks for a moment and then asks, "Mommy?" His mother replies, "What, honey?" and Ben says calmly, "If you want me to hate her, I will." Jackie is speechless, pulling back on her horse's reins.

Despite Ben's jarring honesty at the end, that scene's earlier sarcasm gets laughs, so it is easy to recall and it always sparks lively discussion about how both the child and the parent are speaking in code. Most parents understand that the subtext of "I think she's pretty" to be either "Don't blame Isabel; blame me" or "I don't want you to hate Isabel" or "Isabel has some redeeming qualities" or "I really like Isabel, but you really don't, and that's super uncomfortable."

The subtext of the mother's snarky reply is, perhaps, "I detest Isabel" or "I'm jealous of Isabel's physical beauty" or "Only a fool would find Isabel pretty, so don't fall for it" or "I resent that my ex-husband has dumped me for a younger, more attractive partner." Of course, there are always multiple, plausible decodes of well-written dialogue, as is the case for real-life dialogue. In the workshop, parents generally offer insightful suggestions and enjoy the exercise of decoding *what people say* to extract *what people mean*. In my experience, most parents are good at cracking kids' secret code. Offering empathy is where they stumble.

To frame the third and most challenging question set, I usually ask the audience to imagine themselves magically transported into the movie. "Picture yourself as the benevolent aunt or uncle, riding your own horse alongside the mother and her two kids," I say. "You witness this conversation, most of which is spoken in code. And you're decoding the whole time. You sense the conflict, the tension, which isn't about getting lost or being pretty. Instead, it's about the pain of divorce and of having to share parenting with your ex's new wife." Then I ask, "What could you say—now that you have decoded this conversation—that would provide genuine empathy to both parent and child? What could you say that would help the two of them feel understood?" Suggestions from the audience typically include:

- "Oh, come on, you guys. Let's just enjoy this horseback ride." (minimization + distraction)
- "I'm sorry that you're both still stuck on this." (apology/sympathy + criticism)
- "It's not really about the teeth, is it now?" (therapizing + confrontation)
- "How about we invite Isabel over for lunch tomorrow and everyone can just get to know each other better?" (problem-solving)

None of this is empathy, as you know from the previous two chapters. They are all well-intentioned remarks, but none will help this parent and child feel understood. A few might make them feel even less connected. Sure, they come from a place of caring and concern, but they fail to express compassion and thereby form a connection. They fail to lower the drawbridge by providing genuine empathy. To master **Transformation 5**, we have to figure out how to lower that drawbridge.

WHY THE DRAWBRIDGE GETS STUCK OPEN

At this point in my presentation, a few parents always raise their hands to ask, "Why empathy? Why does every interaction have to turn into a touchy-feely discussion about thoughts and feelings? Why dance around the issue? Why not just solve the problem and move on?" My quick answer to that question is exactly what you remember from Chapter 9: "Because people stink at solving problems when they are upset. Strong emotions cloud thinking—even positive emotions. Empathy fixes that." Yet even after understanding empathy's power, some parents hesitate to use it because they are afraid of saying the wrong thing. Other parents hesitate because expressing empathy exposes inner thoughts and feelings, and that is a vulnerable place. My solution for all this hesitation? A combination of brain science and a recovery plan. That combination gives most parents the courage to try empathy for real. Here is what I say:

"If you front-load problem-solving and toss empathy in later (if at all), then you should expect backlash. Most parents have endured the futility of trying to reason with a distraught child or teenager. It's next to impossible because the overactivity in the emotional center of our brains (the *limbic system*) puts our reasoning center (the *prefrontal cortex*) on hold. Rage, fear, sudden sadness, and other bursts of negative emotion literally shunt the neuronal connections between these two parts of our brains. So, because of how our brains are wired, order matters: Empathy first . . . problem-solving second." For some reason, a neurobiological fact is more convincing than a fiftysomething psychologist. Fair enough.

Next, I say, "For those of you worried that your adjective might miss the mark, that your attempt to empathize fails to accurately describe your upset child's thoughts or feelings, I have some good news: Your kid will still know you care because you are *trying* to understand. You get partial credit. Even better, your kid might *give* you the correct adjective, so you can stop guessing."

Out of a teenager's mouth, such a correction might sound something like this:

> **Meredith:** Did you read your email?! They cut our group out of the program because Mr. Spence doesn't think our lyrics are appropriate!
>
> **Parent:** Oh no. You've all been practicing together for weeks! You gotta be so disappointed.
>
> **Meredith:** No, I'm not disappointed. It's bullshit! Damn, I should have seen this coming!

Just for a minute, ignore the profanity and try to paraphrase what Meredith has said. You might say something like, "OK. I get it now. You're especially angry because you think this was predictable." Now here comes the nearly foolproof part. If "angry" does not capture "bullshit" adequately, you will hear about it, yet get another point (or half point) for trying. However, if your empathic statement is anywhere near accurate, Meredith will offer confirmation, such as: "Yes! Exactly!" or "Finally! Now you get it!" or a pursed-lips smile that is the teenage equivalent of "duh."

Returning to the *Stepmom* example, what would it sound like to provide empathy to Ben and his mother after Ben's plaintive bid, "Mommy, if you want me to hate her, I will"? That depends, because everyone's style is different. Which of these possibilities sounds most natural to you?

- "You're both unsure how to feel about Isabel." (feeling adjective = *unsure*)
- "You're sad to see how the shape of the family is changing." (feeling adjective = *sad*)

- "It's confusing not to know what the future looks like." (thought adjective = *confusing*)
- "You're both wondering whether disliking Isabel is easier than liking her." (thought adjective = *wondering*)
- "Ben, you sound loyal to your mom . . . maybe because you can tell your mom is mad at Isabel." (thought and feeling adjectives = *loyal* and *mad*)

Art may imitate life, but parents' real-world worries seldom involve riding thoroughbreds in the countryside. Far more common for us are settings like cars and kitchen tables and concerns such as: "My kid doesn't listen to me" and "My kid doesn't tell me anything" or "I don't feel like we trust each other" and "It's like whatever I say, my kid does the opposite." So how can you earn respect, not rebellion?

CRAVING CONNECTION

If you want to know more about what your child is thinking or feeling, you have to engage them in more conversations about thoughts and feelings and not let conversations about expectations and outcomes dominate your interactions. You do not need to talk about thoughts and feelings all the time (thank goodness, because it would be exhausting for you, not to mention annoying for your friends and family), nor do you need to make deeply personal disclosures of adult content (thank goodness here as well, because that could feel weird). However, you will need to talk more "head and heart" than usual.

Remember that a relationship is an interactive process where both parties contribute. Try to avoid framing your child's reluctance to engage as "That's the problem with my kid" or, more generally, "That's the thing about teenagers." If you want better and more communication with your child, start by asking yourself, *What do I use communication for?* For example, all parents critique and instruct. Both forms of communication are helpful . . . some of the time. What sets Pressure Parents apart is that they critique and instruct *most* of the time, using communication for judgment far more than connection. Not surprisingly, children and adolescents disengage from relationships where they perceive more disapproval than love or where they consistently fail to achieve their parents' expectations. To reiterate: Kids crave connection. They would rather be heard most of the time than get their way most of the time.

BEYOND CASUAL AND FACTUAL COMMUNICATION

A simple way to improve parent-child communication is to focus on just a few types of messages, such as praise, criticism, and questions. Then, for realism, we can compare how these messages sound when they are superficial (involving casual comments or simple facts) to when they are deep (involving thoughts and feelings). Finally, for clarity, we can choose a single setting, such as a soccer game, where parents and kids interact. **Table 1** provides two examples (harmful and healthy) for three kinds of utterances (praise, criticism, and questions) at four different depths (casual, factual, cognitive, and emotional).

There are a few ways to learn from **Table 1**, the easiest being to read across one of the rows labeled Praise, Criticism, or Question. As you read the short examples in each cell, from Casual to Emotional, you will begin to feel what we mean by **Communication Depth**. Both Cognitive and Emotional types of utterances require speakers to reflect more than they would with a Casual or Factual type of utterance. For example, compare "There will be more practices and other games" (Casual) to "I'd be so angry at myself for losing by so much" (Emotional). There is nothing wrong with Casual or Factual utterances—parents and kids use them all the time—but they lack much power to strengthen relationships and get kids to open up. By comparison, Cognitive and Emotional utterances can unlock even the most guarded kids because talking that way shows your child that you are attentive to their inner experiences.

TABLE 1. HARMFUL AND HEALTHY PRAISE, CRITICISM, AND QUESTIONS

TYPES OF PRESSURE

Harmful:
Parents emphasize outcomes and tend to declare what they and/or the child *must be* or *should be* experiencing. Children typically perceive these declarations as absolute, do-or-die, authoritarian statements.

Healthy:
Parents emphasize effort and tend to share their own experiences and make guesses or empathic statements about the child's experience. Children typically perceive these as understanding, attentive, authoritative statements.

Statements in BOLD occur *more frequently* than their counterparts.

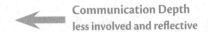

Communication Depth
less involved and reflective

COMMUNICATION TYPE	CASUAL (brief and informal)		FACTUAL (focus on information)
	HARMFUL	HEALTHY	HARMFUL
Praise Example: Child played well and team won the game.	**Hey there, winner!**	Good work out there!	**You're a step closer to being league champions.**
Criticism Example: Child played poorly and team lost the game.	**You could have won easily, but you just gave up.**	There will be more practices and other games.	**Your kick missed the goal by less than an inch.**
Question Example: Child played hard and game ended in a tie.	**Really? A tie?**	Got all your equipment?	**What will it take to win next time?**

Communication Depth
more involved and reflective ⟶

	COGNITIVE (focus on thoughts)			EMOTIONAL (focus on feelings)	
HEALTHY	HARMFUL	HEALTHY	HARMFUL	HEALTHY
I saw you dribble right past their defense.	You knew your team would kick some butt today.	**Your focus allowed you to ignore the heckling.**	I bet now you feel tempted to go for the gold.	**I bet you feel proud of how well you played.**
More spin on the ball might've made it curve in.	You know damn well what it takes to win.	**You lost focus after they scored a goal.**	I'd be so angry at myself for losing by so much.	**Everyone feels bad when they miss an easy goal.**
What's a better way to clear the ball?	Why do you think the game ended in a tie, pal?	**What's a different mindset that might work?**	Can't you see how dejected the team feels now?	**Is it more frustration or surprise you feel right now?**

Another way to learn from **Table 1** is to pick any two cells from the same **Communication Depth** column and compare how they sound. For example, "Hey there, winner" and "Good work out there" are both casual utterances, but the former emphasizes an outcome; the latter emphasizes effort. Or hear the difference between "Why do you think the game ended in a tie, pal?" and "What's a different mindset that might work?" Both refer to what a child may be thinking, but the harmful version again emphasizes the unsatisfactory past outcome, whereas the healthy version emphasizes the effort applied to a future attempt. Most kids would perceive the first question to be sarcastic, even mocking, but perceive the second question to convey interest, even support. Neither the harmful pressure nor the healthy pressure version of this question can suddenly erase the disappointment that a young athlete might be feeling after tying a game they feel they should have won. The goal of adopting the healthy version of any of the utterances in **Table 1** is not instant relief but durable connection. Each time you make the intentional choice to communicate deeply—by referencing thoughts and feelings—and to choose healthy pressure over harmful pressure, you are making an investment in the relationship with your child. That investment pays dividends in three ways:

1. **Better problem-solving.** Your child will be calmer, more creative, and more focused. Therefore, they will be better able to cooperate with you to solve problems.
2. **Better sharing.** Your child will be more likely to open up and disclose details about what they are doing, thinking, and feeling. Therefore, you will know more and worry less.
3. **Better bonding.** By repeatedly investing in interpersonal connection, your relationship with your child will grow stronger, more durable. Therefore, the two of you will more fully enjoy good times and more quickly recover from conflict.

After studying **Table 1**, you will have a keen sense of the difference between healthy and harmful verbal pressure. You will also understand the new concept we introduced in this chapter—communication depth. We recommend using the deeper forms of praise, criticism, and questions intentionally, as a way of applying healthy pressure and accelerating your child's development. In the next chapter, we explain how to maximize the power of praise and use criticism and questions to enhance your child's motivation and performance.

chapter eleven

PRAISE, CRITICIZE, AND QUESTION EFFECTIVELY

How to Communicate Deeply with Your Child

• TRANSFORMATION 6 •

A S PARENTS, WE KNOW THAT WE WILL NOT BE AROUND FOREVER, SO we need our children to grow into insightful, independent adults who give their best selves to others and bounce back from adversity. When we promote our children's development through the skillful application of healthy pressure, we help prepare them for continued success, even in our absence.

Despite the tremendous value of social-emotional learning—from cross-cultural agility and social justice to creativity and compassion—many people still ridicule this work as "touchy-feely" or "soft skills." In truth, social-emotional skills are the hardest for most people to master. Therefore, in the pages that follow, we offer expert tips for improving how you praise, criticize, and question your child.

As we discussed in the previous chapter, verbal communication can be shallow (referring to casual observations or facts) or deep (referring to what your child is thinking or feeling). In addition, verbal communication at any depth can apply healthy pressure or harmful pressure, as our examples in **Table 1** suggested. Like every other suggestion in this book, the strategies we offer in the current chapter are not a rigid recipe for skillful parenting. Instead, they are a collection of sensible tools that we encourage parents to apply flexibly, to fit their style, circumstances, and definition of success.

EFFECTIVE PRAISE

The phrase *effective praise* might sound redundant. All praise feels good and increases desirable behaviors, right? Wrong. Some forms of praise fall flat and do little to shape future behavior. Ineffective praise is typically broad, outcomes-focused, or both. Classic examples are "Good job" or "Way to go." You may truly believe that your child's performance was good or nice, so statements like these can be true. But they are weak because they fail to communicate *what* exactly your child did or *how* they achieved excellence. A theatrical play, for example, has so many different lines, cues, and set changes—some of which may not have gone as planned—that telling your child "Great job in the play tonight" will feel at least imprecise and at worst inaccurate. In either case, it is relatively shallow verbal communication.

Equally ineffective are comments such as: "Awesome A in English" or "Love the marks in math." Focusing your praise on stellar outcomes may make your child smile briefly, but such praise lacks the power to strengthen your relationship or shape their future behavior because it ignores the methods and effort your child used to get the high grades. Herein lies another irony of the Pressure Parent persona. You may intend your praise of positive outcomes to lead to more of those outcomes in the future, but it will not.

The excellent performance at the heart of the positive outcome does feel good to your child, of course, as does whatever recognition they receive. Just remember that grades, trophies, ribbons, and titles are *proxies* for excellent performance. Like paper money, awards *represent* something of value, but they do not have intrinsic value. What does have value and what does feel good is performing well on a test, at a race, in a contest, during a recital, and so on, especially after working hard to prepare and especially if the performance brought joy to other people or helped them in some way.[1] Thus, another reason that praising positive outcomes is less impactful than praising efforts is that your child has already experienced the effort-outcome link and enjoyed the inherent gratification of a successful outcome.

Effective praise, by comparison, has some or all of the Six Ss: Soon, Spontaneous, Sincere, Specific, Striving, and Stand-alone.

- **Soon:** You offer the praise soon after you witness or learn about the good behavior, rather than much later, as an afterthought.

- **Spontaneous:** You offer praise freely. No one needs to prompt you to offer the praise, including your child asking, "What do you think?" Praise lacks potency if the actor has to fish for it.

- **Sincere:** You genuinely feel that your child has put forth praiseworthy effort or accomplished something that, for them, deserves credit. Your sincerity will shine through in your tone, word choice, and body language. Don't feel it? Don't say it.

- **Specific:** You cite details in your praise that prove you were paying close attention. Your attentiveness feels good to your child, and the specifics, especially regarding the methods they used, help your child replicate the praiseworthy action.

- **Striving:** Your praise focuses on your child's effort, rather than the outcome. This builds grit and decreases harmful pressure by shifting focus away from the outcome.

- **Stand-alone:** Your praise is not a prelude to "but," such as "The colorful adjectives made your essay more vivid, but the main character's motivation is still unclear." Both the praise and the criticism here may be accurate. The problem is that phrases beginning with *but* can negate the preceding praise. "You played a great match, but really choked in the last set" or "You followed the recipe carefully, but the bottom of every cookie is burned" are examples of two-part statements where both parts could be true. Unfortunately, the critical *but* phrase in the second half of the sentence erases the praise in the first half. You will have time to discuss mistakes and improvements later, but if you want your praise to mean something now, let it stand alone and sink in. Imagine how much more powerful the praise would feel if you were simply to say, "You played a great match," or "You followed the recipe carefully." Kids usually add their own critique after hearing effective praise, such as: "Yeah, but I really choked in the last set," or "Yeah, but the bottom of every cookie is burned." At that point, you might follow your child's lead and discuss mistakes and improvements. When kids initiate a critique of their own performance, the discussions that follow are usually fruitful and do not detract from the praise you offered.

Offering praise soon, spontaneously, and sincerely gives it the right timing, origin, and tone. When the praise cites specifics, emphasizes striving, and stands alone (without a *but* statement attached), it sticks. To master **Transformation 6**, incorporate as many of these Six Ss as you can, and try to avoid their opposites. **Table 2** has examples of both.

MINDSET

It is important to point out that occasional praise without effective elements is not harmful. However, constant platitudes (the opposite of sincere praise) and generalities (the opposite of specific praise) can contribute to what psychologist Carol Dweck calls a "fixed mindset," meaning a belief that one's talents and weaknesses are unchangeable traits. Dweck's research suggests that young people with a fixed mindset believe that talent alone leads to success and that sustained effort is not required. Consequently, they recognize their intelligence, athleticism, artistic abilities, and other talents for what they *are*, rather than what they *can become* if they worked to develop and improve them.

A young person who says, "I'm not a math person," or "I'm an actor, not a singer," or "I'm terrible with names" clearly has a fixed mindset. Likewise, parents who offer commentary such as: "You're a natural for learning languages," or "Of course you got an A; physics is your thing," or "That's not a school for someone with your intellect" contribute to kids' fixed notions of their aptitude.

By contrast, young people with a growth mindset believe that their learning and intelligence can grow with experience and effort. Parents who encourage healthy risk-taking and who praise effort, rather than out-comes, help nurture a growth mindset. Not surprisingly, young people with growth mindsets put in more time and effort than their fixed-mindset peers, which ultimately leads to higher achievement,[2] not to mention less cheating and reduced levels of harmful pressure. However, teaching young people to adopt a growth mindset sometimes has only small effects on their academic achievement, suggesting other factors are at play.[3] For example, when a student's peers do not value challenge-seeking, the effectiveness of growth-mindset interventions is muted.[4] Therefore, as you study **Table 2**, notice how the six effective elements contribute to a growth mindset *and* consider other reasons why effective praise matters.

Alone or in combination, the Six Ss of effective praise help young people understand and internalize their accomplishments. Praising your child with these elements will motivate them from within because they will attribute positive outcomes to their own healthy risk-taking, planning, and effort, rather than to dumb luck, fixed attributes, or ex-trinsic rewards.

TABLE 2. THE SIX *SS* OF EFFECTIVE PRAISE

EFFECTIVE ELEMENT	EXAMPLE *WITHOUT* EFFECTIVE ELEMENT	EXAMPLE *WITH* EFFECTIVE ELEMENT	WHY IT WORKS
Soon: praise that comes soon after learning about or seeing positive behavior	*You were a fantastic gymnast when you were little . . . so strong and flexible. You were a natural.*	*You were fantastic this morning on the floor exercise . . . so strong and flexible. It must feel good that all your practice has paid off.*	In most cases, the sooner that praise comes after the positive behavior, the more strongly it reinforces that behavior.
Spontaneous: praise that is offered without prompting or suggestion from another person	PARENT 1: *What did you think?* PARENT 2: *About what?* PARENT 1: *Sam's acting talent, silly!* PARENT 2: *Oh. You were great, Sam!*	PARENT 1: *Wow! What a show, Sam!* PARENT 2: *You said it. Every detail.* SAM: *Guys, relax. It wasn't perfect.* PARENT 2: *The audience loved it!*	Unsolicited praise feels authentic because it is voluntary, not obligatory. It is what you *are moved* to say, not what you *ought* to say.
Sincere: praise that is heartfelt in tone, form, and content, not a generic platitude or exaggeration	*You're the best twelve-year-old dancer in the world, I swear. I think you were just born to dance! Just amazing!*	*You and the other dancers impressed me so much with your precise and graceful moves! That clearly took a lot of rehearsal.*	People take original, honest praise more seriously than generic one-liners or over-the-top gushing.
Specific: praise that references details and proves the observer was attentive	*Great speech! I thought I would be bored, but I was actually interested in what you discussed. Once again, I have to say: Good job.*	*I thought the comparison you made between school and summer camp reinforced your thesis about the value of experiential learning.*	Referencing details not only shows you were paying attention but also provides a clear focus for pride.

Striving: praise that focuses on the process, method, and effort, not simply the outcome	*I'm so proud of you for winning Best in Show for your age group. I've already posted about it online.*	*You worked harder for the competition this year than last year, and you deserve to feel enormously proud of your accomplishment.*	Emphasizing effort over outcome helps to nurture a growth mindset. Plus, using "you" instead of "I" increases kids' sense of agency.
Stand-alone: praise that is not immediately followed by caveat or criticism	*You got As in your STEM classes, but an A– in English and a B+ in French. I can't imagine what went wrong.*	*Congratulations on earning As in your STEM classes. I imagine that you studied a ton for your finals. That took lots of self-discipline.*	When criticism follows praise in the same sentence, it makes the praise feel more like a way to cushion the blow than a true compliment.

REWARDS

Extrinsic rewards, such as grades, money, toys, trophies, or likes on social media, do motivate young people, but the effect often backfires soon after one removes the reward. By *backfire*, we do not mean that the positive behavior—the one for which the reward was given—drops to its original level. It completely disappears. The research program of Mark Lepper and his colleagues at Stanford University has demonstrated this repeatedly, beginning in the 1970s.

In one classic study, the researchers randomly assigned preschool children into two groups—one got extrinsic rewards (prizes) for coloring and one was simply allowed to color. Later, when the rewards were removed and both groups of children were given supplies for various activities, including coloring, the group that had been rewarded for coloring did very little coloring. One way to interpret this outcome is that the children in the extrinsic reward group were thinking something like, *If a grown-up gave me a prize simply for coloring, then coloring is probably not a fun activity to begin with. If the prizes have dried up, I prefer to do something else.* Of course, that is not how preschoolers talk to themselves.

However, that was the kids' logic, according to Lepper's studies. When the extrinsic, material rewards disappeared, so did the motivation to perform the activity.

Children who received no money or certificate or prize for coloring had a very different experience. Those kids experienced the inherent, creative joy of the activity. Given the choice among several activities the next day, they often chose to color.[5] The science is clear: Payment kills passion. The lesson for us all is: Do not routinely offer material rewards for any positive behavior that you hope your child will someday do on their own. Extrinsic, material rewards can be used to kick-start a new behavior, such as toileting, but must soon be replaced with extrinsic, nonmaterial rewards, such as verbal praise. Ultimately, a behavior must be intrinsically rewarding to last. In this example, pride or gratification that you can toilet yourself is what keeps that behavior going. Compared to parents who do not offer material rewards, parents who routinely pay their children for getting top grades, give them a new bicycle if they attend summer camp, or allow them to play video games if they mow the lawn will have children with less intellectual curiosity, social courage, and family responsibility. Constantly offering extrinsic rewards also affects the parent-child relationship. Instead of an authentic connection, the parent-child relationship becomes largely transactional.

But wait! Are parents not allowed to give their child something nice to mark an achievement or important event, such as a birthday, a music recital, or high school graduation? Of course they are. These are milestones, not everyday activities, such as homework, instrument practice, and household chores, so the material objects are gifts, not bribes or rewards.

However, even when you give milestone gifts, we recommend that you consider your timing and rationale. The child who receives a beautiful bouquet *the day before* their recital, with a note from their parent(s) that says, "Wishing you all the best for tomorrow's recital! You've practiced your pieces for months and we're excited to hear you play!" will understand that gesture as an expression of love, encouragement, and appreciation for their perseverance. The note focuses on effort and support; the timing makes the gift independent of the outcome. Whether or not the child plays well on the day of the recital, they have already received a milestone gift in recognition of their dedication. By contrast, the child who receives a bouquet *after* their recital is more likely to feel that their parents are rewarding the outcome, as if none of the grit it took to get to that point was worth commending; as if only the final, virtuosic performance was deserving of a reward.

Please do not obsess about gifts you may have given your child in the past. Surely, your child felt your love and admiration. Just consider, in the future, which behavior you want to mark or reward with material objects. Are you rewarding effort or outcome? Your timing and rationale can transform an otherwise tokenistic act into a powerful way to help your child internalize what is best about their character.

EFFECTIVE CRITICISM

Like effective praise, effective criticism and questions require an awareness of your intent as a parent. Are you criticizing or questioning to berate or benefit your child? If your goal is to benefit them by helping them see where they can improve, then you must pay attention to *what* you are criticizing or questioning. Are you aiming at the person, the process, or the product?

Compare these two parental critiques of a teenager who returns home one hour late after being out with friends.

1. "What the hell? Where have you been? Do you realize how late it is? Who doesn't reply to texts or answer calls . . . on the very phone their parents bought for them, no less?! I'm furious!"
2. "I'm guessing your phone died, but I'm unhappy you're coming home an hour past curfew. We agreed that you'd call home if you were going to be more than fifteen minutes late, right?"

In both examples, the parent is upset, as most parents would be. Indeed, raw emotion is an innate, healthy part of our humanity, and expressing it communicates essential information to the people around us. At the same time, regulating emotions and refining how we express ourselves are learned skills that enhance or erode the effectiveness of our communication. Think of raw, negative emotions like a freshly unearthed potato—not particularly appetizing. In fact, it does not look or feel much different from the stones you had to dig up to get to it. Yet if you take that potato and wash it, peel it, slice it thinly, deep-fry it, and add seasoning, it becomes irresistible. The point is, you can deliver your raw emotions to someone, but they might find it so unappetizing that they reject it . . . or reject you. Prepare it properly, however, and the other person is likely to listen and understand. That preparation, that regulation and refinement of emotions, is what many people call *tone*.

In example 1 above, the parent begins with a hostile tone ("What the hell?"), labels the child ("Who doesn't reply . . ."), and impugns the child's character, indirectly accusing them of being a spoiled brat. In example 2, the parent begins by offering an out ("I'm guessing your phone died"), describes her feeling ("I'm unhappy . . ."), references the parent-child relationship ("We agreed . . ."), and attempts to establish some common ground (". . . right?").

Regarding intent, consider whether the parent's manifest goal in this scenario is to berate or benefit their child. (Perhaps it is both. The child deserves a reprimand, *and* the child's behavior must change.) Sometimes, a single piece of effective criticism can deliver two or more messages, but single statements also have a main thrust. The thrust of example 1 is to berate; the thrust of example 2 is to benefit. Consequently, the teen's reaction to the different approaches, and therefore the two criticisms' effectiveness, will be markedly different.

In response to parents berating them, most kids feel attacked and get defensive. They may clam up or snap back—either way, they are likely to reject, not internalize, their parents' underlying concerns. An unproductive period of silence or an angry argument may follow, keeping the level of communication shallow.[6] Berating sometimes seems effective when kids do change their behavior, even temporarily. Yet this is a classic application of harmful pressure—the threat of punishment coerces compliance. The teen in the previous scenario might return home before curfew next time, but it will be to avoid another berating, not because they have understood and internalized their parent's perspective.

At this point, some parents might ask, *Who cares why my kid is following the rules? As long as they're home on time, I couldn't care less what they think about having a curfew.* Indeed, coerced compliance is seductive. It can make parents coerce compliance in other areas, such as academic, athletic, or artistic pursuits. However, what your child thinks *does* matter because durable behavior change is only possible when the child has understood and internalized the concept. Conversely, if the child is behaving only to avoid punishment, they are unlikely to comply when the threat disappears. In this case, if the parents are away for a night, the teen is likely to ignore their curfew altogether. When there is no chance of getting caught, why not stay out all night? If you want your child to behave well even when no one is looking, then you will have to move beyond berating.

Example 2 is likely to be effective because it references the parent's emotions and establishes some common ground. The child is more likely to hear their parent's concerns and might even engage in conversation—if not now, then perhaps the following day. If the teen changes their behavior and abides by the curfew in the future, it will be because they understood their parent's perspective and felt an increased, internal sense of responsibility. Example 2 might now seem sensible, but an approach that references emotions and establishes common ground still leaves many parents asking, *Why can't I just say, "Because I said so!" and get better behavior in the future?* The answer is: Sometimes you can, but durable behavior change is fueled by mutual empathy, not harmful pressure.

In this curfew example, the parent needs to understand that most adolescents strive for independence, love hanging out with their friends, and usually lose track of time when they are immersed in fun activities. For their part, the adolescent needs to understand that most parents feel an enormous responsibility for their child's welfare, crave respect from their kids, and take it personally when household rules are ignored. Achieving mutual understanding is not always easy or straightforward, but when both parent and child see life from the other's perspective—when there is mutual empathy—then positive behavior change happens faster and lasts longer. Even if your child disagrees with you, or you disagree with your child, they will respond better to your criticism when they understand the thoughts and feelings and relationship components that form the basis for your criticism.

CONSEQUENCES

Before we turn to effective questions, we would like to discuss *consequences*, a popular euphemism for punishment. Maybe the parent should ground this kid who missed curfew, take away their allowance, or limit their screen time. Indeed, psychologists and other parenting pundits have written entire books about applying age-appropriate consequences as a way to shape behavior. Most of them say the same thing: Consequences—like criticisms—are effective when they promote understanding and give kids a chance to improve.

Too often, parents punish impulsively, out of anger, without thoughtfully considering whether the consequence they have shouted is instructive or simply unpleasant. In this case, an instructive consequence might be requiring the teen to return home one hour *before* curfew for a month. If they can do that reliably, then the parent could reinstate the regular curfew time. That consequence is likely to work because it logically relates to the misbehavior and it includes a chance to improve. A punishment such as doing the dishes every night for a month has no thematic connection to the original rule violation and provides no opportunity for the teen to demonstrate that they can improve their behavior.

For younger children, we recommend that parents add an epilogue to every consequence. After imposing a time-out or after a logically related punishment, ask your child, "Do you know why you got a time-out?" or "Do you know why we took away screen time for a week?" You might think this kind of post-punishment comprehension question is something only nerdy psychologists ask their kids. However, when you realize how often kids misunderstand why parents are upset or why parents doled out a punishment, you will ask a comprehension question every single time. As fathers, we were both stunned at how frequently our own children misunderstood consequences when they were little. But it is normal. Sometimes, consequences do not make sense to kids because they see the world so differently from how adults do. Other times, kids hear the emotion in parents' voices, become upset themselves, and are unable to follow the parents' initial explanation of why the behavior under scrutiny was wrong. Heck, sometimes kids just forget during the minutes they are in a time-out how they got there in the first place. Again, the importance of understanding a consequence as a prerequisite to internalizing some behavior change cannot be overstated.

A final word about consequences: Their usefulness is limited. Most misbehavior is evidence of a skills deficit, not malice. Children and adolescents are still learning how to behave, and the only thing that punishments teach a person is what *not* to do. For example, if you slap someone's hand as they reach for the plate of cookies you told them not to touch, what have you taught them? Well, you have taught them not to reach for cookies, at least not when you are watching. That is a very specific prohibition under a very narrow condition. Not much of a life lesson. Plus, do you really want to spend all your parenting hours teaching your child what not to do? Our real goal—as parents, as teachers, as mentors, as leaders—is to teach kids what *to* do. We want our kids to learn impulse control, emotion regulation, and the virtue of unselfishness. We want them to think more clearly about the consequences of their actions and to respect others. We want them to become creative problem-solvers, to show some humility and self-deprecatory humor, and to persevere after stumbling. These are long-term parenting goals, of course, and we achieve them one parent-child interaction at a time. Although this is not a behavior management book, we can recommend the work of psychologist Ross Greene for parents who want to rely less on consequences and more on cultivating their child's social, emotional, and behavioral skill set. As Dr. Greene puts it, "So long as caregivers are solely focused on modifying a child's behavior, the problems that are causing that behavior will remain unsolved. But when caregivers focus instead on solving the problems—collaboratively and proactively—not only do the problems get solved, the challenging behaviors that are associated with those problems subside."[7]

EFFECTIVE QUESTIONS

Besides rule-breaking, the most common source of parental criticism and questions is a child's underperformance. When you know your kid could have done better, criticisms and questions naturally blossom in your mind. We suggest keeping those thoughts to yourself (at least for now) and pausing to reflect on your purpose and perspective. The next time you feel that sudden surge of censure, ask yourself the central question of this chapter: *Is my goal to berate or benefit my child?* Chances are, you want to benefit them, so the next question to ask yourself is: *How does my child see this situation?* After that, ask yourself, *How can I help my child understand how I see things?*

Consider this example: Your thirteen-year-old tells you that they have decided to run for class president. You tell them that sounds like an interesting idea and ask whether there is anything you can do to help. They explain that the school forbids parents from helping and forbids students from spending their own money on their campaign. To be equitable, the school gives each candidate twenty-five dollars to spend on marketing materials and supplies. You are reassured by your child's understanding of the campaign rules, optimistic that they will succeed, and impressed by the school's providing an opportunity for self-directed work.

Over the next ten days, you do not notice your child working on the campaign, and when you ask about it, they tell you they have been working on the campaign at school. A day later, you hear from another parent that her daughter won the election, so you decide to ask your child about the outcome that evening. They are disappointed, of course, and confess that they did very little work on this project. You are disappointed as well, but for different reasons. Regardless of the outcome, you know that your child could have put forth more effort. You also feel simmering anger as the criticisms and questions blossom in your head. What next? Try keeping those thoughts to yourself (at least for now) and pausing to reflect on your purpose and perspective. Here is a question checklist, along with some plausible answers:

Q: Is my main **goal** to berate or benefit my child?
A: Sure, I want to benefit them. But I'm also ready to tear into them for their weak effort and for telling me they were doing substantial campaign work at school.
Q: How is my **child seeing** this situation?
A: Honestly, I can't tell whether they're disappointed only about losing or also about their half-hearted attempt at winning the election. Are they as angry at themselves as I am at them?
Q: How can I help my kid understand how **I see** things?
A: I don't know yet, but I'm desperate to have them take future projects seriously and be totally honest with me about their progress. Smart people don't go far in life if they're lazy.

There are other valuable questions to ask yourself before discussing the campaign fumble with your child. If you use the simple checklist above, two great things will happen: (1) you will keep your cool and (2) you will be able to think of some effective criticisms and questions. You already know now what makes criticism effective. To pose effective questions, focus on promoting mutual understanding, which is a hallmark of your Support Parent persona. Avoid interrogation, which your Pressure Parent persona might be tempted to use. Do any of these four interrogation methods sound familiar?

FOUR INTERROGATION METHODS TO AVOID

Leading

Asking a question as a setup to make your point. For example:

Parent: What did you hope would happen in the election for class president?

Child: Um . . . well . . . I was hoping to win, obviously.

Parent: You were hoping. I see. Well, hoping didn't really do the trick, did it? Maybe you should have put in just a little bit of time and effort.

Fact-Checking

Asking questions to gather evidence against your child. For example:

Parent: When I dropped you off at school early on Tuesday and Thursday, you said you were going to work on your campaign. What did you do instead?

Child: Well, I did a little. I mean, I talked with my friends about who else was running.

Parent: I get it. I dropped you off early so you could gossip with your buddies. Awesome.

Asking "Why . . . ?"

Starting a question with *why* can feel more accusatory than starting with *how* or *what*. Rhetorical questions that begin with *why* make kids especially defensive. For example:

Parent: Why do you think you lost the election?
Child: Well, I got the least number of votes.
Parent: Obviously. But *why* did you get the least number of votes?

Asking Yes/No Questions

Asking a question that has only *yes* and *no* as possible answers is one way that Pressure Parents limit and control a conversation. For example:

Parent: Did you think you would win the election if you didn't do anything?
Child: No. But I didn't do nothing.
Parent: Did you—or did you not—tell me just a minute ago that you didn't really try?

When Pressure Parents interrogate their child using these methods and others like them, they might experience a superficial win because kids on trial generally say what their parents want to hear, true or not. A Pressure Parent's goal is to prove their point; their kid's goal is to end the interaction as soon as possible. If you sometimes feel that your child is deliberately shortening phone calls and text exchanges, then try listening more, asking more open-ended questions, and fighting to understand, not to win.[8] Returning to our class president example, here is what that approach might sound like. See whether you can catch all the places where the parent is criticizing and questioning without attacking or interrogating.

Parent: I spoke with Grace's mom today, and she said Grace won the election for class president.

Jordan: Yeah. I was going to tell you.

Parent: It's probably not something you want to talk about.

Jordan: Not really.

Parent: What was it like to hear the election results announced?

Jordan: Disappointing. I don't want to talk about it.

Parent: You felt discouraged.

Jordan: Yup.

Parent: How did you run your campaign?

Jordan: What do you mean?

Parent: Well, I didn't see you working on it at home, so I don't really know what you did after I dropped you off early at school. But there is always something to learn from a loss.

Jordan: I probably should have done more.

Parent: More . . . ?

Jordan: Yeah, I don't know. More posters, maybe. More talking with other kids. More just . . . thinking about and publicizing what I would do for the class if I did get elected.

Parent: So one reason you think some of your classmates didn't vote for you is that they didn't know what voting for you would get them.

Jordan: Kinda. I mean, Grace was all about improving the food in the cafeteria.

Parent: That's a pretty clear platform. Something students care about. And Grace got her message out there?

Jordan: She did.

Parent: What was your campaign message?

Jordan: I didn't really have time to put one together.

Parent: You're saying that you could have come up with a clear pitch if you'd had more time?

Jordan: Yeah. Well, no. I probably had enough time—I mean, everyone had the same amount of time. But I, um . . . I kinda ran out of time. I didn't mean to. I just didn't realize how much work it was to run for something, for an election I mean. I thought it was just like, "Hey, you're my friend, so vote for me."

Parent: (doing their best to empathize) I guess it's pretty shocking to discover that it wasn't just a popularity contest. Or maybe to discover that you're not as popular as you thought. Or maybe that big projects take serious work over many, many days. Now you know why I asked whether you wanted my help.

Jordan: (becoming upset) But you weren't *allowed* to help! Parents weren't supposed to help. What could you have possibly done? Let it go, already. I lost, OK? I lost. I learned my lesson. I'll never run again. Are you happy now?

Parent: Whether you run for something again is up to you. But in my mind, the lesson here is not "Don't run again," it's "Run smarter next time."

I get that parents were not allowed to help directly, but I could have listened to your campaign plan. Maybe if you had started to explain your plan to me, you would have realized that it wasn't realistic or detailed enough. You might have been able to make a list of all the stuff you needed to do.

I can always listen, you know. You're smart, but that's only half of it. You also need a plan—a detailed schedule—and the desire to put that plan into action.

Jordan: Well, yeah. I get that now.

Parent: Look, we're both disappointed that you didn't win, but we know *why* you didn't win. I also think you and I are both disappointed that you didn't work harder on the campaign.

Jordan: Are you mad at me?

Parent: Yeah, I am, but not because you didn't win. I'm unhappy that you asked me to drive you to school early four days last week to work on your campaign, but that's not what you were really doing. I feel like you took advantage of me. I wanted to help, but I'm not feeling so generous right now.

Jordan: Yeah. Sorry.

Parent: I hope you'll be honest with me next time, especially if you realize you've run into a problem or a bigger challenge than you anticipated. I said it before, but it would definitely *not* have been against the campaign rules for me to listen to what you were thinking and feeling. What made it hard to tell me what was really going on?

Jordan: I don't know.

Parent: I don't know either, but I hope you can share more with me in the future. And if there's something I'm doing that makes it hard for you to share stuff with me, please tell me.

Let me say one other thing: I feel good that you learned something important about how to handle the next big project you take on.

Jordan: Mmm. I don't know.

The Support Parent here is exerting some healthy pressure by offering genuine praise, constructive criticism, and open-ended questions—all designed to promote the child's understanding of what happened and lean on the parent-child relationship to learn how to do better. If this parent felt tempted to impugn the child's character or interrogate them on the facts, she resisted. Yes, the parent expressed her anger, but in a respectful way. Because this teen did not feel attacked, they engaged in a productive discussion, even after saying early on that they did not want to talk about the election results. There is much more for this parent and child to discuss, but a series of brief discussions, with time for both people to think in between, is usually more productive than a marathon interaction. Even though lots of parents are good at long, moralizing lectures, kids hate them.

Your child will not always engage in substantive conversations, even when your praise, criticism, and questions are thoughtfully constructed. The sample dialogue above is idealistic. But as parents, we must play the long game and stack the odds in our favor by persevering. Remember that sudden behavior change mostly happens in dreamy movies with uplifting scores. Real life is bumpy. We must take comfort in the knowledge that our kids feel our loving attempts to connect, even when they do not reciprocate. Just how involved parents should get in their kids' lives—as they work to connect and to nurture—is the focus of the next chapter.

chapter twelve

BE THE BELIEVER

How to Trust Your Child to Succeed
and Avoid Being a Space Invader

• TRANSFORMATION 7 •

HEALTHY NEWBORNS HAVE REFLEXES, INCLUDING SUCKING AND grasping, that help them survive. Sometime between six and eight months after birth, most babies start grasping objects, putting those objects in their mouths, and sucking on them. Objects such as wooden blocks, plastic toys, or one's own toes provide no nutrition, but sucking on them provides lots of information on taste, texture, firmness, and response to getting wet. Infants do not learn by studying textbooks, discussing current events, watching documentaries, or hiking in the wilderness. Someday, they will. But as infants, they learn in other ways, such as looking, listening, and—yes—sucking on almost everything they can put in their mouths. If a parent sees an infant grasp or start to suck on something that might harm them, the parent intervenes by invading their space and taking the harmful object away. That is what any caring adult would do. We involve ourselves in children's development to prevent harm, promote learning, and express our love. The tricky part after infancy is knowing not only how but also *how much* to involve ourselves.

The younger a child is, the more appropriate it is that we do things for them, such as feeding, toileting, bathing, and clothing them. As they get older, we typically let them do more on their own. We even celebrate certain milestones of independence, such as walking, being potty-trained, and tying shoelaces. How much adults do for kids and how much kids do for themselves depends partly on the lenses and prism in **Figure 2**, which we introduced in Chapter 4. How much we do for them also depends on their social, emotional, and cognitive development, which are not part of **Figure 2**. Developmental level (maturity and ability, but not chronological age) must now factor into our model of parental pressure, because optimal parental involvement hinges on it. For example, children with profound neurodevelopmental disorders might need an adult to help them dress for their entire lives, whereas neurotypical children can dress independently by the time they are between four and six years old.

As **Figure 2** describes it, Relational Pressure ranges from involved (healthy) to intrusive (harmful). But how can a parent determine optimal involvement? Simply knowing that it ranges or that its optimal level changes according to a child's maturity and ability is interesting but not helpful. Fortunately, the research on parental involvement has yielded several practical findings, the most important being this: Optimal parental involvement is something only the child can report, based on their lived experience.[1] For example, consider two single-parent families, each with one child. The two parents may treat their child identically, but one child may report that this level of parental involvement is optimal, whereas the other child may report that the exact same parent behaviors feel intrusive or over-involved. The subjective nature of optimal involvement can make it seem elusive to parents, but this chapter will help you find the optimal level and intensity of involvement. A case example is a great place to start.

Mr. Bergil returns home from running errands on Sunday afternoon and remembers that his fourteen-year-old son, Croix, has a trumpet lesson and a math test on Monday. Without knocking, Mr. Bergil enters Croix's bedroom and finds him on his phone. "Let's see it," says Mr. Bergil, holding out his right hand, palm up. "C'mon, buddy. Hand it over."

Croix sighs in protest. "Dad, I'm right in the middle of texting my math group."

"Good," replies Mr. Bergil. "I hope it's about math," he adds, peering at Croix over the rims of his reading glasses.

"It is," states Croix.

"Let's see," repeats Mr. Bergil, wiggling his fingertips. "You know the rule. As long as I'm buying your phone and paying the bill, I reserve the right to look at it anytime, for any reason . . . or for no reason at all."

Croix slowly places his phone in his father's hand. Mr. Bergil studies the home screen carefully, navigates through a few apps, reads some text strings, and then hands it back. "Croix, I don't see anything in your group chat about studying for math. Most of this is about someone—your classmate, Drake."

"Dad," Croix says, smiling, "Drake is a . . . No, no, forget it. There's nothing in there about math yet because we were *just about* to set up a time to Zoom. But then you walked in."

"Mmm-hmm. OK. But I want to be part of that," insists Mr. Bergil. "I told you that we were going to go over math and run through your newest trumpet pieces today. You've got a test tomorrow and a lesson tomorrow evening."

"Dad, I'm all set. I'm fourteen . . . thank you, but . . . I mean I appreciate your help, but I'm fine studying for the test and practicing by myself," says Croix.

"That's what you said last time, and I'm pretty sure you remember what you got on the last math test," Mr. Bergil points out.

"Dad, nobody did well on the last math test," explains Croix. "I told you why. Mrs. Lopez put questions on there about stuff we hadn't even covered yet," explains Croix.

"Exactly," Mr. Bergil says calmly. "Which is why you and I are going to go over this unit together *and* start working on the problem set for the next unit."

"What?!" exclaims Croix. "So when am I gonna have time to practice trumpet and do my other homework? It's not like we can just do the next whole math unit in, like, fifteen minutes."

"Well," says Mr. Bergil, "that's something you should have thought of Saturday morning when you were kicking around a soccer ball in the park with your friends."

After an awkward silence, Mr. Bergil continues. "You need to learn to budget your time and plan ahead. Fortunately, I'm here to do that for you. But someday, you'll have to manage your schedule yourself. Right now, it seems to me like we have to get cracking. Show me your assignment book, and we'll map out the rest of the day."

. . . .

Reading this, you might think Mr. Bergil is either lovingly attentive, annoyingly invasive, or somewhere in between. On the one hand, he remembered Croix's obligations for the following day, monitored the boy's phone use, set aside time in his schedule to help Croix study, and set high expectations for Croix's performance. On the other hand, Mr. Bergil did not knock or ask to come in; he asked for the boy's phone without considering what he was interrupting; he overruled Croix's request to study alone and with his classmates—insisting instead to be part of the online study session; and he micromanaged Croix's schedule.

Two parents could consider this one example and pin it to opposite ends of the Relational Pressure scale. Yet, where a parent pins it does not matter. Only one person can accurately say whether Mr. Bergil's involvement is lovingly attentive, annoyingly invasive, or somewhere in between: Croix. This is a classic case of *intent does not equal impact*. Sure, some of Croix's words and actions make it seem as if he does not appreciate his father's approach, but that does not guarantee how he would answer if a neutral third party asked him to anonymously characterize his father's involvement as too much, too little, or just right.

Transformation 7 begins with accepting that whatever *you* think about your involvement in your child's life, you still need to ask your child to know the truth. What you perceive as an ideal approach may be one that your child perceives as overbearing or distant. You will not know until you ask . . . and the answer might sting. As Prince Hamlet famously lamented, "There's the rub." The good news is that understanding more about Relational Pressure puts you in an excellent position to take a step back in some parts of your child's life and take a step forward in some others. If you can set aside your assessment and listen carefully to how your child experiences your involvement in their daily life, then you will be free to apply just the right amount of healthy pressure, in just the right way, just where your child needs it most.

PARENTAL INVOLVEMENT DEFINED

One can measure parental involvement in two ways: involvement **level**, which is how most parents think about it, and involvement **intensity**, which is how kids think about it. Involvement **level** is composed of all the time, energy, and money that a parent invests in specific spheres of their child's life, such as providing food, shelter, clothes, education, athletic activities, artistic pursuits, social events, and entertainment. You increase your involvement **level** when you do things like shop for groceries, clothes, and school supplies; host birthday parties, sleepovers, and play-dates; attend games, meets, matches, recitals, and teacher conferences; help with transportation to practices, lessons, and the library; and when you encourage, coach, interact with, and worry about your child. If you had a magic watch and wallet set, you could actually measure the time and money you spend on your child. It is much harder to measure the energy you exert on behalf of your child, but you feel it, of course, and it often feels quite gratifying. In any case, the sum of time, money, and energy equals involvement **level**. It is 100 percent parent-made, for which you deserve both credit and gratitude.

Involvement **intensity** is how your contributions and participation *feel* to your child. Does Croix feel invaded, smothered, nurtured, encouraged, or neglected? We would know if we asked our children, but we rarely do. Why? Because as parents, we mistakenly believe either that involvement **intensity** is irrelevant (e.g., *Who cares what kids think?*) or that our involvement **level** is already at the ideal **intensity** (e.g., *I know how to run the show, and I'll tell you when enough is enough*). Still, all parents who have ever criticized their child for acting entitled know firsthand that a high **level** of parental involvement sometimes goes unnoticed or unappreciated—proof positive that what our kids feel (or do not feel, in some cases) does not always correspond to what we are doing. The same is true for all parents whose children have ever yelled, "Get out of my life!" or "It's none of your business!" or "You're ruining everything!" Our children hurt our feelings with directives and accusations like these, but it can be valuable feedback.

On the under-involved end of the continuum, children might complain, "You don't even care!" or "You're just pretending to be interested!" or "You would know if you ever bothered listening to me!" Paradoxically, under-involved parents may feel involved, but not act involved, particularly in their child's eyes. For example, parents who attend their child's events (e.g., games, matches, meets, recitals, exhibits, performances, graduations) yet spend considerable time on their smartphones could say, "I'm a dedicated parent because I go to most of my child's events." However, their child might say, "I wish my parent cared more, but they spend half the time on their phone." As a parent, you are a force in your child's life that weaves in and out, in different ways and at different times. Knowing how to weave in and out with keen awareness of how your child experiences that involvement is an art, not a science. Fortunately, science gives us a practical place to start refining our approach.

Most studies of parental involvement have focused on academics or sports, a few on performing arts. Researchers have generally collected involvement **level** data from parents, involvement **intensity** data from kids, and objective measures of performance from schools, such as grade point average or athletic ranking. The results might seem predictable or too vague to be useful: Kids who perceive high involvement intensity (a kind of harmful pressure) experience more anxiety and perform less well than kids who perceive moderate involvement intensity.[2] And although most studies do not include indifferent or neglectful caregivers, those findings are equally predictable: Most young people who perceive sparse parental involvement tend to experience psychological distress, performance problems, and low self-esteem.[3] Intuitively, you could have guessed that both very high and extremely low involvement are harmful. Perhaps now it also seems intuitive that kids, not parents, are best at determining involvement intensity. Why, then, is something intuitive so challenging for so many parents? The trope of the overbearing parent existed long before the Tiger Parent label. So, what is the story?

HELICOPTERS VS. TANDEM SKYDIVERS

Helicopter parents, as you learned in Chapter 6, hover protectively over their children. By comparison, over-involved caregivers kick Pressure Parenting up a notch by acting in ways that feel uncomfortably intrusive to their children. Here are some sports analogies: If helicopter parents coach loudly from the sidelines, over-involved parents actually run onto the field and start playing. Over-involved parents and their children are like tandem skydivers, where the experienced instructor is strapped to the student's back. The instructor guides the student through the whole jump, from airplane exit through free fall, piloting the canopy, and landing.[4] This brand of high-touch guidance is completely appropriate for infants (and novice skydivers), often appropriate for toddlers, sometimes appropriate for school-age children, and rarely appropriate for adolescents. In sum, high-touch guidance is most appropriate when maturity or ability are minimal, especially when the activity risk is high. Chronological age is never what determines optimal parental involvement. Yet because maturity and ability tend to increase with age, we sometimes oversimplify the involvement equation when we think that younger kids need more parental involvement and older kids need less. A more accurate thought is: *Parental involvement tends to be high when activity risk is high, or when maturity and/or ability are low.*

I (Chris) would want an experienced instructor strapped to my back the first time I tried skydiving, regardless of my age. The activity risk is high, and my ability is low. (My maturity has always been questionable, but that's a different book.) Later, once I had learned, practiced, and mastered the basics, I would want the instructor to get off my back, literally and figuratively. Were the instructor to remain strapped to my back long after I felt ready for my first solo jump, I would feel smothered. Of course, feeling ready and being ready are not the same. This is where maturity kicks in—for the professional instructor to explain why I needed more instruction, and for me to accept their recommendation. The point is: As soon as I was truly ready for my first solo jump, I would yearn for independence and eschew tandem jumping. Were the instructor to skydive next to me, as a step toward eventually letting me skydive solo, I would feel excited, competent, joyful, and confident. I would enjoy the gratifying glow of budding self-reliance.

At the other extreme, if I had never skydived before and someone strapped a parachute to my back and dumped me out of a plane, I would panic. Indeed, that level of under-involvement is abusive. Fortunately, the extremes of feeling smothered or panicky are not the only two options for our kids. Russian psychologist Lev Vygotsky (1896–1934) named the sweet spot between over-involvement and under-involvement "the zone of proximal development." He said that optimal learning happens when someone with more skill than the learner—such as a parent, teacher, coach, or talented peer—provides just enough supportive instruction to keep the learner interested and challenged.[5] Giving no instruction could leave the learner feeling abandoned, frustrated, or confused; doing everything for the learner could leave them feeling bored or smothered. Perhaps, if Vygotsky were alive today, he would add that moderate parental involvement—which avoids the extremes of over- and under-involvement, as perceived by the child—helps parents and children enjoy more time together in the zone of proximal development.

PARENTING IN MODERATION

The less mature or able a child is, the easier and more ethical it is for a parent to step in and be highly involved. For example, parents spoon-feed or hand-feed infants who are ready for solid food. In the domain of "baby feeding," parents do not ask; they just step in, feed the child, and everyone is happy. The parent-child boundary here is what psychologists call *permeable*. The parent can pass through it easily, at any time, to act in the best interests of the child. And in this case, stepping through that permeable boundary does not feel invasive to the child.

As time passes and the child's coordination grows, most parents do let children feed themselves, perhaps after offering a bit of physical or verbal instruction. A parent's having taken a step back in the domain of "baby feeding" is a great example of nurturing a child's autonomy. In fact, parents who are ambivalent about letting toddlers feed themselves are likely to get pushback. Trying to feed a toddler who has learned to feed themselves usually backfires in the form of flailing arms, pursed lips, and cries of

"Me!" This protest suggests that, in the domain of feeding, the parent-child boundary is not so permeable anymore. Generally, it is harder for a parent to step in, uninvited, and do something for a child of any age when that child has already gained some independence in that area. Maturation and ability decrease the permeability of many parent-child boundaries.

You can use the concept of boundary permeability to find the optimal level of parental involvement. Forget about making a list of what you can and cannot do for your child. Just start by reflecting on what things your child already does independently. Then ask yourself, *How frequently do I step in and do this thing for my child, without being invited?* Another way to ask this question is: *When do I treat this parent-child boundary as permeable even though there is no longer a reason to?*

Of course, your answers to these questions depend on what domain of competence you are reflecting on. For example, a parent might feel perfectly free to offer unsolicited advice to their teen who is learning to drive (the "novice driver" domain), somewhat free to step in and provide guidance on a cookie recipe that the teen has followed successfully before (the "junior baker" domain), but not at all free to tie that teen's shoelaces for them (the "dressing" domain). The first boundary is permeable, the second semipermeable, and the third impermeable, except in the cases of injury, illness, or cognitive impairment. Optimal parental involvement varies accordingly.

Parents of older children and adolescents need just as much self-awareness as parents of younger children, but they get free coaching from their kids. (The sass is also free, but far less helpful.) In particular, most adolescents reliably let parents know when they have crossed, or attempted to cross, an impermeable boundary. For example, your teen might be happy to have you drive them to the movie theater to meet some school friends, but unhappy if you decide to park and walk in with them. And forget about chatting with their classmates. One of our parent friends tried this once and recounts the blunder like this:

. . . .

INSTEAD OF DRIVING UP TO THE FRONT OF THE CINEMA, I
parked in a spot close to the entrance. Everything seemed fine, but
when I turned off the car, my kid asked me, "What are you doing?"
I said I was parking because I had to use the bathroom and I didn't
think I could hold it for the twenty-five-minute ride home.

When I started to get out of the car, do you know what my kid said?
"Wait. Please. Just hold it. You can hold it. That's what you always told
me. Seriously, you can't just walk in there with me." I was astonished.

I tried to downplay the whole thing by telling my kid they were being
silly and reminding them that I knew most of their friends already. I
said that I would just wave, say hello, and not to worry—I wasn't
going to watch the movie with them . . . I was just walking in to use
the bathroom.

Then my kid said, "See what I mean? That's so embarrassing. Seriously,
my friends don't want to know that you have to go to the bathroom!"

I was about to give my kid a lecture on entitlement and tell them
to hitchhike home, but then it dawned on me: All these objections
had nothing to do with me or my biological needs at the time. The
issue was my kid's being able to showcase their independence to their
friends by walking into the theater alone.

. . . .

All parents have made similar missteps, much to the mortification
of our teenagers. Going forward, however, the more you can catch yourself in the act of eclipsing your child's opportunities for autonomy, the
better. The more you can take a step back, the more comfortably your
child's independence will grow. That makes great sense, but we still have
not directly answered the question about why letting go and giving your
child some developmentally appropriate freedom is so hard for Pressure
Parents. There are at least three related reasons.

RELATIONAL PRESSURE PARADOXES

1. The Trust Paradox

Every parent wants their child to reflect some admirable parts of themselves. Every parent also enjoys the vicarious pleasure of having admirable parts of their child reflected in them. Just think of how easy it is for parents to brag, whether it is "Cameron learned how to walk!" or "Cameron got into UCLA!" Sometimes, however, these reflections are more than flattering sparkles on the dappled surface of parental identity. Sometimes, a parent's identity is inextricably entwined with their child's identity, a relationship pattern called *enmeshed*. The paradox for enmeshed parents is that whenever they trust their child to act independently in some way, they find it nearly impossible to step back because distancing themselves from their child equates to letting go of part of their own identity. This **trust paradox** causes children in enmeshed parental relationships to experience bouts of harmful relational pressure and significant delays in the development of their independence.

2. The Role Paradox

Human babies are born helpless, as are the babies of many other species, but human children stay dependent on their parents for more than a decade. Evolutionary biologists believe that this unusually long timeline is necessary for humans to develop our complex thinking and language skills. Whatever the explanation for children's protracted reliance on adults, the result is that we parents end up feeling pretty darn important. In fact, we are indispensable, at least for a while. However, if we lose sight of how necessary it is for children to become self-reliant, then we do risk depriving them of their autonomy. The **role paradox** is that by enthusiastically embracing our essential role as providers and protectors, we parents may have trouble updating our role as our children mature. Rather than demonstrating our belief in children by granting them age-appropriate freedoms, some parents come to believe that their child cannot *ever* succeed without them. In turn, this belief becomes parents' rationale for staying over-involved. Parents caught in the **role paradox** communicate the message to their children that active parental participation is required for success. Not only does this belief make children anxious when their parents are not at their side, it also fuels a kind of over-involved behavior that robs children of many opportunities to figure things out and make important decisions on their own — two skills they will need for personal success and for contributing to the survival of the species.

3. The Failure Paradox

A derivative of the trust and role paradoxes is the **failure paradox**. Parents whose child forms the core of their adult identity tend to see their child's failure as their own. If the child fails a French test, the parent feels as if they themselves also failed the test (or at least that they failed as a parent). Although this belief is false, it fuels parental over-involvement by spawning the thought: *If I had been more hands-on during homework sessions and test preparation, my child and I would not have failed.* After inserting themselves even more intrusively into the child's French studies, the parent in this example will see any future improvements as evidence that a high level of involvement is essential to the child's success, thus perpetuating their over-involvement. And if the child performs worse on future tests, a parent caught in the **failure paradox** will think, *I'm still not doing enough*, and may become even more over-involved. To be clear, parents' academic, artistic, and athletic coaching can be extremely helpful, as long as parents do not see their child's failure as their own.

Many parents can see a shadowy reflection of themselves in one or more of these paradoxes. Whether or not you do, the last section of this chapter offers some practical strategies for involving yourself in your child's life at a level they will perceive to have near-optimal intensity.

To work best, the things you say and do must be authentic. When you put our suggestions into practice, remember to put them into your own words.

OPTIMAL INVOLVEMENT

1. Believe in your child

Whatever their strengths, weaknesses, illnesses, and idiosyncrasies, your child will be happier and healthier, enjoy more autonomy, demonstrate extra resilience, and achieve greater successes if they feel certain you love and trust them. Believing in your child, regardless of their temperament, attractiveness, or intelligence, is essential to their well-being.[6] Sample phrases that express belief in your child are:

- I will always love you, no matter what.
- I believe you can achieve great things if you work hard at it.
- This doesn't change how much I believe in you. Everyone fails some of the time. Successful people, like you, think about and learn from those experiences.
- You've got great skills, and you can learn more. I'm always happy to help or connect you with someone who can help.

2. Grant decision-making control

As with everything else we have advocated for in this chapter, allowing your child to make independent decisions is something parents must finesse according to their child's developmental level. In practice, the principle is the same across all stages of development: Provide just enough guidance to allow the child to figure things out for themselves. Whenever possible, do not directly or completely solve problems *for* kids or give advice *to* kids without their asking for it. A few excellent autonomy-nurturing questions are:

- What do you think needs to happen next to figure out this problem?
- What are some different ways you might solve that?
- What are the pros and cons, from your point of view?
- What is your previous experience telling you about making a smart choice?

3. Ask permission

This might seem like a role reversal, but each time you ask for permission, you not only give your child a chance to make a decision, you also demonstrate your belief in their burgeoning wisdom. At some point, you can expect an angry response if you fail to ask permission in circumstances where most parents in your culture would ask. Hence, this approach can also reduce parent-child conflict. Some common examples are:

- Would you like some more? (after noticing an empty plate)
- What do you want to watch? (after your child sits down while you're watching TV)
- May I come in? (after knocking on the bedroom door)
- Who would you like to invite? (after finding a time for a birthday party)

4. Leverage mistakes

We learn more from mistakes than from successes, so it would make sense to engineer more failure experiences for our children. Lucky for us parents, kids make enough mistakes on their own that we just need to spot the built-in lessons. What takes practice is resisting the temptation to start the lesson with shame. As alternatives to "You should have . . ." or "What were you thinking when you . . .," try adopting a calm tone and asking questions such as:

- What parts do you think you missed along the way?
- How would you do things differently next time?
- What did you figure out along the way?
- What are you seeing now that you didn't see as clearly before?

5. Ask for feedback

As we emphasized earlier in this chapter, parents must learn how their kids *feel* about the intensity of their involvement. Sometimes, older children and adolescents will offer their parents unsolicited feedback on involvement, as we mentioned earlier. Most of the time, with most kids, you will have to ask for feedback. Good questions to try are:

- Which parts of this would you rather have done on your own?
- How did you feel about my helping just now?
- Next time you do this, what role, if any, would you like me to play?
- How can I be most helpful next time a situation like this happens?

6. Manage your anxiety

Easier said than done, but equanimity is something for all of us to work on continually. As we noted in Chapter 8, negative affect can be contagious, and nobody performs their best in a state of extreme emotional arousal. Therefore, the more you can temper your expression of high anxiety, the better your child will perform. (Both you and your child are likely to feel better, too.) Some effective (and free!) ways to manage your anxiety include stepping away from the situation for a few minutes; getting a good night's sleep; practicing regular meditation; enjoying physical exercise; focusing on what you can control, rather than what you cannot; avoiding the pitfall of taking your child's behavior too personally; and sharing how you feel with a calm, trusted peer.

7. Listen to other, trusted adults

Your spouse, partner, relative, coworker, clergy, close friend, or therapist might give you a perspective that helps you see where you are over- or under-involved in your child's life. Sometimes, hearing this feedback is hard, but all parents lose sight of their own parenting from time to time. Like fish who cannot (in theory) make sense of the question "How is the water?" because they are immersed in it, we cannot always provide an accurate or complete answer to "How is my parenting?" All parents benefit from another adult's perspective on their approach—whether or not that adult is a parent themselves. Of course, you do not have to agree with or follow that other adult's recommendation. (That said, acquiescing to your in-laws until their visit ends has great diplomatic value.)

8. Find additional sources of pride and joy

We thought about calling this strategy "Get a life," but we figured that was too sarcastic to be professional. Feel free to throw this book across the room now, if you want. But when you pick it back up after a few days, we hope you will have realized how important it is for all parents to have sources of pride, joy, and self-esteem *in addition to* their children. Nothing will ever mean as much to you as your child or children. True facts. Also true is that spending time with a hobby, entrepreneurial project, community service, artistic pursuit, sports club, spiritual practice, or musical instrument will supplement the wonderful work you do as a parent. Bonus: Those supplemental sources of pride, joy, and self-esteem also provide pressure-relief valves that reduce over-involvement and other kinds of unhealthy parental pressure.

chapter thirteen

OPEN YOUR MIND AND YOUR HEART

How to Repair the Damage Caused
by Sociocultural Pressures

• TRANSFORMATION 8 •

ROUGHLY 17 PERCENT OF HIGH SCHOOL STUDENTS IN THE US have seriously considered suicide sometime in the past year, and completed suicides are the second leading cause of death for twelve- to nineteen-year-olds in this country.[1] As if those figures were not frightening enough, consider that youth whose gender identities are not their natal sex[2] or whose sexual attractions[3] are not straight are three times more likely to contemplate suicide[4] and five times more likely to attempt suicide,[5] compared to their cisgender,[6] straight peers. One cause of these severe mental health problems is pressure—pressure to conform to social, religious, and cultural norms; pressure to get summer jobs, internships, and team captainships; pressure to be accepted by peers; pressure to achieve academic greatness;[7] and, particularly caustic, pressure to meet parental expectations.

You probably remember from **Figure 2** (which we hope you have now bookmarked in Chapter 4) that **Culture & Tradition** is the first lens through which parents' instinctive drive to protect their children passes. So rather than condemn other parents or let them cavitate from guilt, we urge you to peer closely into that lens. Armed with a greater understanding of the sociocultural sources of pressure, parents can contribute to local, national, and global movements that support children's healthy development. We recognize that every parent has unique strengths and limitations. Therefore, the goal of this chapter is to inspire you to use your unique strengths to diminish the intensity of at least one of the sociocultural sources of harmful pressure that impinges on the young people you care most about. That is **Transformation 8**.

QUEER YOUTH AND THE PRESSURE OF CONDITIONAL LOVE

There is no more harmful type of parental pressure than conditional love. "I love you as long as you're straight" is an example of conditional love. Worldwide, many youth who are lesbian, gay, bisexual, transgender, transsexual, queer, questioning, intersex, asexual, or pansexual (LGBTTQQIAP, sometimes abbreviated LGBTQ+) experience the soul-crushing effects of conditional love. To make matters worse, the harmful effects of bullying, discrimination, and assault these youth experience at school are especially hurtful without unwavering parental love as a backstop. One recent meta-analysis (a study that pools data from other well-designed studies) found that suicide risk was 2.9 times higher for sexual minority youth than for heterosexual youth, primarily because of episodes of homophobia, violence, and victimization.[8] Of course, other factors are associated with an increased risk for mental health problems, such as poverty, trauma, and race-based discrimination,[9] as we will discuss later in the chapter. For now, imagine a typical week during which a young person who identifies as LGBTTQQIAP overhears one classmate tell another, "This book is so gay"; or overhears their parent comment to a friend's parent, "Can you believe it? I don't know how *I'd* react if *my own* child told me he was trans"; or listens to their teacher tell a homophobic joke to the class with an affected lisp; or has a parent redirect them to "not buy *that* shirt" in favor of "something more masculine" or "something more feminine"; or is berated by their coach to "take off your skirt and man up!"

Too often, unhealthy pressure to conform to romantic, sexual, or gender expression norms goes unnoticed because it is subtler than a parent's vocal insistence on certain clothes, gestures, careers, or choice of partner. Even when it is obvious, it may go unnoticed because parents are preoccupied with their child's academic, athletic, or artistic achievement. Yes, you deserve credit if the first twelve chapters of this book have inspired and guided you to modulate the pressure you apply in these three traditional domains. Nevertheless, your work to eliminate harmful pressure is not over yet. Your child, or one of their young friends, feels an intense pressure to conform to contemporary norms (familial, social, cultural, religious, or other) around their gender identity, gender expression, romantic attraction, and sexual attraction.[10] At times, it might seem overwhelming to stay current with updated definitions and fresh ideas, but liberating our children from harmful social constructs is part of our job. For example, well-publicized movements to eliminate toxic femininity and toxic masculinity have taught parents new ways to update their old concepts of identity, thereby decreasing one kind of intense pressure to conform socially. Despite good progress, a wide range of implicit and explicit biases persists around many aspects of identity.

Before joining a movement, however, all parents must start with some self-reflection. Unwittingly, many parents have said or done (or *not* said or done) things to their children that conveyed *conditional love*. If your child understands your stated or implied message as *I will withdraw my love if some aspect of your identity does not conform to current norms or to the norms I espouse*, that creates problems. For example, one parent we know recalls her mother having remarked, when she was fourteen and fairly certain that she was bisexual, "I wouldn't be unhappy if you told me someday that you were gay, but I would be disappointed. No prom, no son-in-law, and no grandchildren. I would still love you, but to be perfectly honest, I would be sad."

Talk about harmful pressure. The statement *I would still love you* can only be interpreted as superficially unconditional—like something the mother said to make herself feel better. The phrase *I wouldn't be unhappy* is quite different than *I would be happy* and foreshadows the next phrase, *I would be disappointed*. We cannot count the number of friends and clients with whom we have spoken—those in their sixties and those in their teens—who have hidden some aspect of their core identity out of fear of rejection. Paradoxically, their parents believed—like the mother in the example above—that they had made a loving, inclusive, depressurizing statement. In fact, in children's eyes, they had done the opposite by saying, "If the objects of your romantic and sexual attraction do not conform to my hopes and expectations, then my loving feelings toward you will shrink and change." (Perhaps as frequently, straight people's parents criticize them for dating someone whose status, ethnicity, weight, education, wealth, or religion feels mismatched.) Equally painful would be hearing, "If your thoughts, feelings, and expressions of maleness or femaleness do not match the current cultural norms associated with your natal sex, then my feelings toward you will shrink and change." Said more simply, "If you're not straight or if your gender does not match what's between your legs, then I'm going to have a tough time."

We recognize that many cultural traditions, religious beliefs, and laws are based on adherents' interpretations of sacred texts as forbidding certain sexual pairings. We also know the mental health research on how applying these cultural traditions, religious beliefs, and laws can affect young people, at least in Western Hemisphere democracies with developed economies. As we summarized earlier in this chapter, the mental illness and mortality rates associated with LGBTTQQIAP prejudice are bleak. Therefore, we respectfully but categorically disagree with the parts of any law, policy, belief, or practice that treats any person or group as "less than" other persons or groups.

Whatever you may have thought, said, or done in the past, your next task to reduce harmful pressure could be to declare yourself an ally, starting with your child and eventually extending to their friends and your young relatives. In this context, an *ally* is someone who supports LGBTTQQIAP people and human equality in its many forms—both publicly and privately. In the eyes of LGBTTQQIAP youth, it is not enough for adults to adopt a passive approach to discrimination by saying, *I'll do my part by not telling any more gay jokes*, or *I contribute to human rights by having a friend who is lesbian or by knowing another parent whose child is transgender.* Those are positive but passive steps. What LGBTTQQIAP youth need are true allies who take an active approach to human equality and justice by supporting LGBTTQQIAP youth and youth-serving organizations. If this is your calling, perhaps you will begin by speaking up when you hear or read slurs. Perhaps you will donate time or money or participate in antidiscrimination rallies. Some allies spend time lobbying for legislative change in one of the thirty US states that still lacks (as of 2021) comprehensive sexual orientation and gender identity protections. Sometimes, being an ally means supporting resources, providers, and spaces that affirm and assist LGBTTQQIAP youth, especially in rural areas.[11]

For parents raised to believe that LGBTTQQIAP people do not deserve equal treatment under the law, becoming an ally is a big ask. Start small. If a parent you know is struggling to accept their child's romantic or sexual attractions, the best place to start ally work is simply to listen. If that parent is you, seek out a trusted peer who will listen to you in the manner we describe in the next paragraph. Whichever side you are sitting on, remember that empathy, not argument, is what shocked or shaken parents need first and foremost.

In Chapter 9, we made the point that empathy is not agreement, so try to ignore differences of opinion if you are supporting another parent whose child is LGBTTQQIAP. It can be enormously difficult for any parent to wrap their mind around an unexpected or newly revealed part of their child's identity—a part that feels incompatible with some aspect of their own identity, at least initially. Fortunately, empathy helps upset parents feel understood. In turn, feeling understood helps parents show compassion[12] toward their children. It may even prevent parents from disowning their children. If your empathy prevents a young person from being abandoned, that is a triumph—a victory over conditional love.

Consider data from the Ali Forney Center, a queer youth crisis center in New York City. In 2020, the center reported that "more than 80% [of kids we serve] are kicked out of their homes for being who they are," with the rest running away from "abuse, neglect, or a combination of rejection and abuse."[13] Additional factors are always part of the complex circumstances that lead a parent to kick their child out of the home, including the parent's mental health, but this data from the Ali Forney Center suggests that the child's identity plays a huge role. The report goes on to note that many queer youth are further marginalized, with 90 percent lacking insurance, 20 percent testing HIV-positive, and 75 percent having a history with the police. Outside of big cities, LGBTTQQIAP youth living in rural areas experience even higher rates of bullying, discrimination, and bigoted language at school based on their sexual attractions or gender identity.[14] It is nearly impossible to fathom the intensity of unhealthy pressure these young people must feel to hide their identity when *family membership* and *actual survival* are at stake. And for all of them, conforming is not the only source of harmful pressure. In the next section, we review some of those other risk factors.

RACIAL, ETHNIC, AND CULTURAL PRESSURES

At schools, camps, and other youth-serving organizations we have visited in the US, Canada, the UK, Australia, South America, and China, students who identify as Black, Indigenous, or People of Color (BIPOC) have recounted painful episodes of both blatant racism and implicit bias, wherever they are in the minority. Sometimes, these episodes occur in their home country; other times, they occur in a host country. For example:

- Black students walking down a small-town New England street hearing some local teenagers holler, "Go back to Africa!" as they drive by.
- Latinx teenagers waiting in line at a US government office being called "illegals" by some older white people waiting behind them.
- Aboriginal Australian students on a field trip to Canberra seeing *Abo Dogs* scrawled on the inside of a bathroom stall in a fast-food restaurant.
- Taiwanese children attending a summer program in mainland China being ridiculed for their Taiwanese Mandarin accents.
- First Nations students in eastern Canada describing their lobstermen fathers being shot at with flares by white lobstermen.

Sadly, overt racism and xenophobia hurt kids all over the world, every day. Less visible but even more destructive is the insidious, institutional racism of the sort Ta-Nehisi Coates warns his son about in *Between the World and Me*, such as DWB—Driving While Black or Brown. Despite there being many excellent and ethical law enforcement officers in the US, the racial profiling of BIPOC individuals, such as disproportionately higher rates of traffic stops of BIPOC drivers compared to white drivers, has been clearly documented in parts of the US.[15] To avoid, endure, or survive racially beset encounters requires nearly constant vigilance, which adds an exhausting, stressful, inescapable dimension to the other sociocultural pressures BIPOC youth feel.

Most recently, the world has seen the egregious, lethal violence perpetrated against BIPOC individuals by US law enforcement officers who are either under-trained, incompletely equipped, or unaccompanied by another professional, such as a social worker, with a complementary skill set. In particular, lethal police violence against unarmed Black men and women has incensed broad swaths of the population in the US and abroad and brought anti-Black racism into sharp focus. To be clear, the chronic distress caused by institutional racism is not parental pressure. Rather, it is a menacing, invalidating type of identity pressure to which many parents are bystanders. We include it in this chapter because BIPOC parents and children experience this brand of harmful pressure and because all parents—especially those with the most privilege—have a responsibility to understand it and actively work to end it.[16]

Sometimes, parents are more than bystanders. For example, overt and harmful parental pressure enters the race-ethnicity-culture equation when caregivers encourage BIPOC youth to lighten their skin or otherwise conform to an identity expression that does not reflect their authentic self. Consider this first-person narrative from Audrey Noble, a Filipino American woman living in the US:

> I was nine when I received my first—and last—skin-lightening product. It was a black bar of soap gifted to me by an aunt who was visiting from the Philippines at the time. On the label, it promised to exfoliate dead skin, fade away dark spots, and lighten my skin. "You're so dark," she said. "This will help." I was confused, but as a dutiful Asian child who always respects her elders, I smiled back and thanked her. After my aunt's visit, I found the soap in my shower, which I took as a not-so-subtle hint that I should start using it. I remember the soap's black suds lathering and smelling nicely, but no matter how much or hard I scrubbed, using it every day proved futile: I didn't get any lighter.[17]

According to Noble, about half the population in Korea, Malaysia, and the Philippines uses some kind of skin lightening treatment. Use is even higher in India (60 percent) and some African countries, such as Nigeria (77 percent).[18] This harmful pressure is big business. In India, for example, skin-lightening products represent 50 percent of the skin care market and are a $450 million–$530 million industry.[19] Yet change is afoot. Some African countries, such as Rwanda and Ghana, as well as Japan and Australia, have banned skin-bleaching agents because studies on their efficacy are often inconclusive, and many of the ingredients are quite dangerous.[20] White youth typically do not experience this brand of identity pressure, but many BIPOC youth feel it from media, peers, and parents. (Skin-based identity pressures that white and BIPOC youth share in common include clear skin versus skin with acne; clear scalp versus scalp with dandruff; and uneven facial skin tone versus even tone. Each of these dermatological conditions also has a lucrative industry behind it.) Of parental pressure, Noble writes:

> I recently asked my mom about the whitening soap. While she admits that she should've thrown it away, she insists my aunt was coming only from a good place. "Your skin shouldn't be a barrier, but you know how things are," she said. "Family will always want to do everything to even out the playing field for you."

Lighter skin is often a marker of privilege, even within darker-skinned ethnicities—a phenomenon known as *colorism*. Sometimes, colorism is inverted, with darker skin carrying more in-group status than lighter skin. Black students with lighter brown skin than their peers or mixed-race Asian students who try to join campus affinity groups are sometimes told, "You're not Black enough," or "You're not Asian enough," to join. Despite race being an artificial construct, skin color remains a reliable source of prejudice around the world. Interestingly, light skin is sometimes meaningless. As the Yugoslav Wars between 1991 and 2001 illustrate, light skin does not reliably inoculate people against violent, intergroup discrimination. Indeed, genocides throughout history have used ethnicity, religion, and nationality, as well as race, to justify discrimination and death. Historians and sociologists have made compelling arguments that fear, greed, ignorance, alienation from nature, and economic crises fuel the creation of out-groups and in-groups that lead to prejudice, discrimination, slavery, and conflict.[21] Perhaps the battle humans have been waging the longest is to recognize our common humanity. We are making slow, uneven progress, and more work lies ahead. Lest systemic racism and global conflict overwhelm you (as if parenting isn't overwhelming enough sometimes), we now return to the more manageable topic of parental pressure and the role you can play in staving off harmful sociocultural influences.

PARENTS AND MEERKATS

Young people are not the only ones whose performance suffers under great pressure. Many parents experience unrelenting professional pressure.[22] Many feel competitive pressure from other parents, continually strategizing to help their children access or acquire what they perceive to be limited resources. A glance back at **Figure 1** in Chapter 3 could be enlightening if you reflect on the pressures *you* feel, rather than those your child experiences. Keep in mind that **Figure 1** is seven dimensions of *parental pressure*; therefore sociocultural pressures are not included. But now you know they can be just as healthy or just as harmful, including for parents. For example, moms and dads of children who are members of traditionally underrepresented minorities may find themselves in similar positions of constant vigilance for discriminatory racial, ethnic, cultural, and legal forces. For all parents, any unhealthy sociocultural pressure can cause tremendous distress, which can impair parenting quality and, in turn, amplify harmful pressure on kids. Parents who are not functioning at their best are more likely to exert harmful pressure directly on their children, sometimes without realizing it. Overstressed parents are also less able to protect their children from external sources of harmful pressure. Fortunately, we have one another—a global community of instinct-driven caregivers who can support more than just our own offspring.

Think of every good contribution you make to the health and well-ness of the communities beyond your immediate family as a reduction in harmful pressure. Your altruism—in thought, word, or deed—helps other parents be their best selves, which helps their children, which helps your child or children. It is fascinating to realize that the parental instinct to promote our children's positive development is not always manifest as direct parent-child interactions. Sometimes, we protect our children by doing what we can to reduce pressures that may prey on other parents. This assertion may seem paradoxical, especially in competitive communities and cultures. But consider the animal example of meerkats, a type of mongoose found in arid southern Africa (and made hilariously famous by Timon in *The Lion King*). The meerkat example of altruism is sometimes misconstrued as an example of unselfish behavior that comes at a cost to the individual. While the rest of the colony is foraging, one member—called a sentinel—stands guard and alerts the rest of the colony if a predator is near. It may seem that sounding the alarm puts sentinel meerkats at great risk of being targeted and eaten by the predator, not to mention that they are not foraging, so they may go hungry. However, biologists have observed that sentinel meerkats assume duty after eating (so they are well fed) and they are the first to hide from the predator (because they were the first to see it).[23] Contrary to conventional wisdom, sentinel meerkats engage in altruistic behavior that is *not* costly to them as individuals. Indeed, it is beneficial to all.[24] Similarly, parents' efforts to reduce the intensity of harmful sociocultural pressures benefit *both* the community *and* them as individuals *and* everyone's children.

WHEN PRESSURE ON PARENTS TRICKLES DOWN

Advocating for our children and promoting the development of their best selves requires using every tool in this book, along with keeping your family's important traditions alive, building your social support network, and actively struggling against racism, sexism, phobia of differences, damaging beauty standards, and every other pernicious form of prejudice and discrimination. As demanding as these struggles are, they deserve every parent's participation, each according to their ability. The more we let sociocultural pressures interfere with our healthy parenting, the more they can damage our child's robust self-concept. With harmful pressure originating from so many places, most parents feel a strong moral obligation to love and celebrate all the healthy, prosocial aspects of who their child *is*, rather than how they look or who they love.

As valid and virtuous as that previous sentence may be, we recognize that expressing unconditional love toward your child is difficult at times for every parent. We have also treated enough neglected, rejected, and abused children to know that some parents struggle mightily with their caregiving responsibilities. Usually, mental illness and adverse life events, rather than malice, explain these instances of child mistreatment. Consider Andy:

- -

"I LEARNED A LOT DURING MEDICAL LEAVE," ANDY OFFERED. It had been a year since I last saw him, but just a month since our phone conversation to discuss his readiness to return to boarding school.

"That was clear this summer," I said. "You matured so much in how you cope with stress."

"Pretty much anything would have been better than cutting on myself, right?" Andy smiled. I smiled back, knowing how hard he had worked in therapy while living at home and enduring his parents' frequent bickering.

"I remember how worried you were about returning home; how mad you were at me for favoring a medical leave."

"It's all good, Dr. T. You know that. I probably needed a med leave harder than any other student you've ever seen." Andy was still smiling, but I could tell the implicit question was serious.

"You needed it, yes. But I can't make comparisons. I will admit to being worried about what it would be like to return to Carlton and live with your parents, without your older brothers there to provide support."

"Hellish, really," said Andy, smile gone. "My mother kicked me out of the house three times."

"She what? Really? You know you could have called your local therapist . . . or called me . . . we could have helped somehow." I was truly shocked, given how both of Andy's parents had pledged their support for intensive treatment of his depression.

"Oh, yeah. You forget my circumstances, Dr. T. My oldest brother is the Golden Child; my middle brother was, like, my parents' insurance plan; but I'm not even the frickin' insurance plan. Every time my mother kicked me out, she would make it real clear that I was a financial burden and a source of shame. In my family, you just can't be a C student, let alone a C student with depression. You know that one day when I told my mother I felt suicidal, she literally yelled at me that I was just saying that to make her feel guilty."

. . . .

It is hard not to judge parents like Andy's mother. Her brand of harmful pressure is not simply about Andy being better but about being someone else . . . or maybe about not being there at all. How a young person survives such pressure requires a look back at **Figure 2**, which depicts the transformation of parents' instinctive energy to protect.

What helped Andy survive was learning what was in his mother's **Family History** lens that had so badly contaminated her instinctive energy to protect him. Three months into his medical leave, at the peak of one verbally venomous attack on Andy's existence, his mother had revealed the pressure her own parents had put on her to marry Andy's father for social status and economic security. She then claimed that Andy's father had insisted she scuttle her career aspirations to raise two children. And she tearfully confessed how the father had pressured her for a third child—Andy—the day she proposed returning to the work-force. For the first time in his life, Andy understood that his mother loved him, but deeply resented what he symbolized to her. His existence was a ball and chain around her ankle that represented the father's culturally sanctioned dominance and the patriarchal dousing of her professional hopes and dreams. Whatever changes Andy's mother may or may not have been able to make in her own life, she literally saved his by sharing her story. Perhaps some parents reading this case example can reduce harmful pressure on their child by sharing what is in their **Family History** lens.

UNHEALTHY PRESSURE FROM SOCIOECONOMIC STATUS

Although some mental health and behavior problems are more prevalent in higher-income families,[25] children from lower-income families are at greater risk for a host of problems.[26] In large part, this is because parents above a certain income level can purchase more access to resources for their children, compared to parents below that income level. Necessities and resources such as nutritious food, quality health care (including mental health care), excellent educational opportunities (including IDEA 2004 services), and extracurricular activities all cost money. And although money does not buy happiness, it does grant access to supports and opportunities that are associated with happiness. Conversely, parents who struggle to provide for their families experience economic pressure, which, in turn, causes negative changes to parents' mental health, relationships, and parenting quality. Broadly speaking, a reduction in disposable family income is a risk factor for children's mental health.[27] Narrowly speaking, a family's socioeconomic status (SES) has some unusual effects on parental pressure.

First, once a family's SES is substantial enough (somewhere north of the poverty threshold) to provide access to decent nutrition, health care, education, and extracurricular activities, additional income is not associated with higher levels of happiness.[28] What does boost happiness at higher income levels is having a positive attitude, such as being grateful for what one has, rather than jealous of what one does not have.[29] Parents who convey the message that a family members' value *as a person* would be higher if the value of their bank account were higher are unintentionally putting unhealthy pressure on their children. Saying, "I'm sure that being a teacher could be rewarding, but the pay is garbage," or "I know you could major in French, but I don't know what your starting salary would be," or "Your friend landed a job with a six-figure salary? That's what I call success!" all equate goodness and affluence. Expressions such as "Bill Gates is worth more than $115 billion" only reinforce the notion that worth and worthiness are synonymous. They are not. All parents must help kids understand that fact.

Second, SES can hinder or help parental involvement. Many of the lowest-SES families have one or more parents who are working two or more jobs. Traveling to games or performances, attending parent-teacher conferences, and helping with homework are impossible luxuries for parents caught in this dilemma. At the other SES extreme, some affluent parents may become too busy or self-possessed to involve themselves in their child's life in healthy ways. Problems with unhealthy parental pressure exist at both ends of the socioeconomic scale, for different reasons. To understand these reasons better, future research linking SES to unhealthy parental pressure must consider the intensity of parental involvement, as well as parental expectations. For example, our clinical experience suggests that even when parents do not explicitly state their expectations, some low-SES kids feel tremendous pressure to secure a high-paying job so they can *lift up* their family's SES. And some high-SES kids feel tremendous pressure to secure a high-paying job so they can *uphold* the family's elevated status.

Parents at every socioeconomic level can diminish unhealthy (and sometimes unspoken) parental pressure by speaking honestly with their children about how the size of someone's bank account is not a measure of their success or worthiness. Parents can also model the expression of gratitude, even for the small things in life. And at every SES, the subtle ways parents lead by example can be more powerful than only talking about core values. Here are some questions that might help you assess your leadership-by-example in the realms of money and status:

- When you are with relatives, do you gush as lovingly about your child's character as you do about name brands, favorite shows, or celebrity shenanigans?
- When you are with friends, do you express as much admiration about your child's acts of kindness as you do about others' weight loss, clothes, hair, shoes, cars, and other gear?
- When you are with your child, do you spend as much time talking about how their day went as you do playing on your phone, checking texts, and answering calls?
- When discussing choice of school, major field of study, or career aspirations with your teen, do you focus more on their passions or on their earning potential?

If we are honest with ourselves, we all can think of a few ways that our behavior appears to link the value of a person to the status or price of an object. Advertisers are notorious for reinforcing this spurious link. And although there is much to appreciate in the material world, we can intentionally modify the time and talk we expend on *things* so that the *people* who matter most to us always know why they do. When we succeed at loving people more than things, we lessen some of the social and peer pressures that gnaw incessantly at our children.

WHEN PRESSURES ARE LAYERED

Intersectionality is a modern sociological term that describes the overlapping dimensions of a person's identity.[30] These dimensions can overlap to create unique systems of both privilege and discrimination. For example, Johavi is a Latvian Jewish immigrant who identifies as a bisexual young woman. Understanding her lived experience at a public school in southwest Texas must begin by considering the intersection of her nationality, religion, immigrant status, sexual attractions, gender identity, and geo-cultural environment. Complicated, indeed, even for Johavi. Perhaps especially complicated for her parents to understand, given the similarities and differences between their own intersectional identities and hers. Less complicated is outlining how her parents can apply healthy pressure while avoiding as much harmful pressure as possible.

Like most other adolescents, Johavi will experience some peer pressure to experiment with alcohol and other drugs, to become heterosexually active, to conform to fashion and media trends of the time and place where she lives, and to adopt whatever attitude toward school her majority-group peers express. How her parents discuss these peer pressures with her, the attitude they adopt toward the family's circumstances, their acceptance of her intersectional identity, and their understanding of her lived experience as different from theirs will all contribute to either healthy or harmful parental pressure. We all remember social and peer pressures from our youth, but our children are experiencing strikingly different variations. A case example helps illuminate intersectionality at work.

Imagine Johavi's parents are always talking anxiously about her father's undocumented status, the threat of deportation, and the specter of Immigration and Customs Enforcement (ICE) breaking up the family. They will unwittingly increase the pressure Johavi feels to keep to herself and stay out of trouble, lest she call attention to her family. This may leave her socially isolated and feeling lonely. If her mother keeps asking her, "Have you met any nice Jewish boys at school?" then she will unwittingly increase the pressure Johavi feels to be straight and to marry within her faith. This may leave her feeling depressed. And if her father often badgers her with a specific, high-stakes outcome, such as, "Just keep getting As so you can get yourself into medical school," then he will unwittingly increase the pressure Johavi feels to study late into the night and to ignore her passion for robotics. This may leave her feeling anxious, unfulfilled, or even hopeless.

Social pressures are complex because identities have so many overlapping dimensions, as Johavi's story illustrates. At times, social pressures feel intractable, which causes kids, clinicians, and caregivers to feel helpless. Compounding those feelings of helplessness for parents is the fact that parents do not create or amplify many of the social pressures their children feel. However, parents can reduce their contribution to harmful social pressures in two ways: (1) express a broad definition of success; and (2) ask thoughtful, open-ended questions.

Look back two paragraphs at the comments Johavi's mother and father made and you will see how narrow their definition of success is. Johavi will be successful if she is heterosexual, interested in marrying a Jewish man, and able to achieve superior academic marks, attend college or university, complete medical school, and become a doctor. Of course, all this must happen while she struggles against delinquent peer pressures and intermittent sexism, manages her anxiety about her father's citizenship, and suppresses her passion for both females and robotics.

Johavi's parents are observant and concerned, but also proud and unaware of her inner struggles. They notice that she often appears gloomy, yet they assume her countenance indicates fatigue from working so hard in school, a behavior for which they praise her regularly. Sadly, they have no idea how lonely, depressed, and anxious she feels. They also have no idea how much they contribute to those negative emotions. Most parents do not know half of their child's experience of the world because they avoid asking, perhaps because they worry that the answers will be painful to hear; perhaps because they worry they might be implicated.

In Chapter 11, we described effective questions as having an openended format, with a focus on thoughts and feelings. (Remember that casual and factual questions, as well as a lot of simple, yes-no questions, are generally less effective.) Of course, good questions from parents do not always garner a response from your child. If you can gently persist, children do eventually respond with information about their social and cultural experiences in the world—with classmates, teammates, teachers, coaches, clergy, store clerks, employers, and police, to name a few. Your child might even dish about their love life. (Probably not, but you can always hope.)

STEMMING THE TIDE

The racial, ethnic, cultural, economic, social, and peer pressures young people feel come through a variety of pipelines: social media and other websites; hallways and locker rooms; malls and movie theaters; parks and sidewalks, to name a few. Racial, ethnic, cultural, economic, social, and peer pressures come from other places, too. But wherever kids hang out with other kids, two factors amplify pressure: (1) the presence of advertising and (2) the absence of adults. Parents have precious little influence over the pipelines themselves, but we do control our own behavior. Therefore, to conclude this chapter, we offer ten ways to thwart the pernicious pressure coming through the Internet and all the non-virtual spaces where kids hang out with other kids.

1. **Remember the Good.** A great deal of what young people experience when they interact with their peers is healthy. Parents' wholesale criticism of social media, video games, or other aspects of popular culture serves only to distance children from their parents and handicap parents' ability to discuss and contextualize the messages to which children are exposed. (See Tip 2, next.) Moreover, because technological advances and ubiquitous social media enable constant, often distressing comparisons, all young people need a trusted adult to keep encouraging them to be *their* best, not *the* best. (See Chapter 7.) Children of all ages benefit from their parents' genuine praise of their prosocial behaviors and personal accomplishments.

2. **Discuss Media Content.** Ask your child how they are spending their time with peers and about the content they are consuming and disseminating. Especially important are discussions about advertising, which you can prompt with open-ended questions, such as: "What are some of the products that you see advertised?" "What message is the parent company trying to convey?" "What attributes does this ad suggest are most valued?" "How does this message make you feel?" "What sort of pressure do you and your friends experience to be like the people in the advertisement or to buy what you see?" and "What is implied about what's going to happen to you if you use this product or service?" In our experience, it is more productive to ask these questions casually, on a regular basis, in different relaxed settings. Announcing that you want to have a sit-down talk with your child about the media they are consuming is a recipe for reticence.

3. **Respect Cultural Differences.** Parents and children who spend time in two or more cultures will appreciate many rich contrasts. They will also experience the stress of clashing values. Parents who are mindfully respectful of cultural variations in language, touch, politeness, discipline, relationships, and the arts are less likely to impose home-country values and traditions in coercive or traumatic ways. And within the same country, culture, and family, observance of religious and cultural traditions can differ markedly between generations. This difference can result in parents' criticism or flat rejection of their child's romantic interests. Of course, you may see your child's choice as disrespectful, just as your child may see your denunciation as disrespectful. Whenever religious differences are generating uncomfortable pressure, our first recommendation is to initiate a series of conversations with one or more clergy members that you and your child both trust.

4. **Limit Extracurricular Activities.** Overextension is the condition of being stretched too thin because one believes the credo "I can, therefore I must."[31] Because most high-achieving schools do not limit extracurricular activities, parents must discuss reasonable limits with their children. Excessive commuting, overflowing schedules, sleep deprivation, insufficient study time, insufficient playtime, painful trade-offs, and other consequences of overextension all put tremendous strain on the parent-child relationship and undermine the essential support that you are trying to provide.

5. **Engineer and Encourage Shared Leisure Time with Peers.** Genuinely close relationships are the primary source of resilience, of happiness, and of peak performance.[32] In addition to peaceful face-to-face time with you, your child needs in-person time with their friends.[33] Arranging this can be as simple as speaking with other parents to find times when different families can get together or as complex as helping your child brainstorm and then schedule, weeks in advance, some in-person leisure time for them and some of their friends. Whatever it takes, and however non-spontaneous it feels, in-person leisure time is healthier than a steady diet of superficial interactions over social media.

6. **Redefine Success.** Ask yourself how you have defined success for your child. The narrower and higher-stakes your description is, the more harmful the pressure. Revisit previous remarks you have made and consider a broader definition, focused on effort and discovery. Share your updated definition with your child. Begin discussions about your new view of success by owning your old definition, such as, "I know I used to talk about how much I think you'd like going to the university I attended, but the more I think about it, the more I realize that this is your education, not mine. Yes, my alma mater is in the media a lot, but so are lots of other

schools. Whether a school is mentioned in a magazine article or not, whether your classmates are applying there or not, whether you've even heard of the school before . . . none of these things is as important as whether the school is a good match for you. I just want you to have a fulfilling experience."

7. **Pick Your Poison.** Look again at **Figure 1** and do some honest self-reflection on those seven categories of pressure. Remember that each of these seven constructs could be poisonous or positive. For example, ask yourself what you think and how you feel about competition. Is it intense and aggressive or gracious and cooperative? How does your view align with the media and cultural customs to which your child is exposed? What about your attitude toward control? Is this the sole purview of parents, or could you share some decision-making control with your child or teen? How can you weave developmentally appropriate decision-making into your family's traditions? Consider a small, healthy change you could make in just one of the constructs in **Figure 1**. That is a fantastic start.

8. **Clean Your Lenses.** Look back at **Figure 2** and do some honest analysis of the powerful energy that emanates from your instinct to protect your child. How does that energy change as it passes through the lenses of Culture & Tradition, Family History, and Individual Identity, as well as the prism of Temperament & Personality? What factors outside the family support your parenting values? What factors detract or distort those values? Some non-parental sources of pressure may be immutable; others may be malleable, as we discussed earlier in this chapter. Consider what you can add, change, or remove to help you be a stronger Support Parent. And remember the meerkats. The positive influences you have on your extended family, your neighborhood, your child's school, and the larger community will return to benefit you and your child someday.

9. **Swallow Your Bias.** Parents apply harmful pressure unintentionally by making comments and asking questions that have bias baked in, such as: "I think that after you go to college, get married, and have kids, you'll understand what I mean," or "Are you going to the prom with Suzy?" Did you catch all of the baked-in biases? Rather than assuming your child is straight and plans to conform to cultural norms, try constructing unbiased versions, such as: "I think that after more life experience, you'll understand what I mean," or "Are you planning to celebrate with friends?" You can also gently revise the comments and questions from adult friends and relatives, whenever you deem them biased. For example, next time Uncle Seamus or Aunt Polly asks your male child, "Got a girlfriend?" or asks your female child, "Got a boyfriend?" you can speak up and say, "What Uncle Seamus is asking is *Any romance in your life?*" or "What Aunt Polly means is *What's new in your social life?*"

10. **Visit with Other Parents.** Sociocultural pressures, especially those resulting from discrimination, trauma, poverty, and high-achieving schools, are too daunting for parents to face alone. The social support that comes from getting together with other parents, giving and receiving empathy, sharing ideas for healthy child-rearing, and simply relaxing is revitalizing.[34] And when your batteries are recharged, you are a better parent—one who can offer great support to a pressured child.

Modifying the verbal, nonverbal, and relational pressure that you apply to your child is the central task of this book and—as we acknowledged in the Introduction—it is hard work. Your reading to the end of Chapter 13 shows your strong commitment to that work, even when the pressures emanate from sociocultural places far outside your family circle. In the next chapter, we offer some concluding, concrete guidance on how to apply our eight parenting transformations.

chapter fourteen

PUSH WITH PROWESS

The Unlikely Art in Action

WHAT HAS TRANSFORMED THE PARENTAL INSTINCT TO PROTECT into a corrosive force? The sharp focus on a narrow set of high-stakes outcomes. Around the world, loving parents have unintentionally made their children miserable by describing opportunities as scarce, competition as fierce, and perfection as vital. Parents intensify harmful pressure with urgent tones, invasive control, and displays of personal worth that spotlight material wealth. The result is a cohort of young people who are anxious, depressed, and unmotivated—precisely the opposite of what parents intend. Tragically, some young people feel so distressed, ashamed, and hopeless that they end their own lives.[1] Whatever paradoxical contribution we are making to our children's suffering, we bear a responsibility to undo. Of course, there are always other factors at play in children's development—some even more influential than the parent-child relationship. Our hope is that this book energizes all parents to contribute what they can, when they can, to their child's health and happiness.

STOP BLAMING CULTURE FOR EVERYTHING

Blaming contemporary cultural trends for all harmful pressure is folly, especially when we cannot punish culture or teach culture to act differently. Indeed, blaming culture alone is the most hackneyed straw man on the nonfiction bookshelf. But there is a reason those books are on the shelf in the first place: Blaming culture sells, because blaming culture is safe and easy. It is easy to write and easy to read; it feels safe to shift the blame away from us, as individuals, and instead to condemn something vast and impersonal that can be inherently classist and systematically racist.

In writing *The Unlikely Art of Parental Pressure*, we have intentionally sidestepped the pitfall of placing 100 percent of the blame for our children's pressure-induced suffering on culture. Yes, we devoted the previous chapter to repairing the damage caused by sociocultural pressures. After all, parents are the most influential speed bump between culture and children, so we share a responsibility to filter and contextualize what our kids are exposed to. In addition, we share a responsibility to eliminate biases, prejudice, discrimination, and maltreatment, all of which augment harmful pressure. Every other chapter in this book focuses squarely on parents because we—our children's primary caregivers—are the entities most empowered to steer our kids in a healthy direction by applying healthy pressure.

PIVOT POINTS

Applying healthy pressure hinges on your embracing three core concepts. Each concept reveals a way to pivot from your Pressure Parent persona to your Support Parent persona:

1. Heaps of pressure do not enhance performance

Contrary to popular belief,[2] additional self-imposed and external pressures, past a certain point, actually impair performance.[3] (This phenomenon is the thesis of Hank's book, *Performing Under Pressure*.) When parents reject these scientific findings, they trip into the Performance Paradox and adopt their Pressure Parent persona. By contrast, we can pivot to our Support Parent persona by:

- emphasizing persistently strong effort, rather than a specific, do-or-die outcome (Transformation 1);
- encouraging our children to achieve their *personal* best, rather than to become *the* best (Transformation 2);
- including the galaxy of possibilities in conversations about who our children can be, rather than perseverating on the traditional few that fit convenient categories (Transformation 8); and
- dreaming broadly with our children about what they could do educationally and professionally, rather than limiting discussions to the exclusive options with international recognition (Transformation 8).

2. Parents know best, but they do not know everything

If you want to know more, you must ask. When it comes to understanding your child's inner life, you must ask. When it comes to knowing whether you are being invasive, you must ask. When it comes to appreciating your child's authentic identity, you must ask.

When parents believe that intuition and experience will tell them all they need to know, or that asking is not worth the trouble when they already know best, they trip into the Intention Paradox and adopt a Pressure Parent persona. By contrast, we can pivot to our Support Parent persona by:

- expressing genuine empathy (Transformations 3 and 4);
- listening for the subtext of what our children say (Transformation 5);
- using praise, criticism, and questions that reference thoughts and feelings (Transformation 6); and
- asking our children how they experience our parenting (Transformation 7).

3. Your history is not your child's future

We all bring traditions, innovation, successes, failures, and (for some) trauma to our job as parents. We also bring our culture(s) and other aspects of our identities, such as gender identity, gender expression, race, nationality, ethnicity, sexual attraction, romantic attraction, and (for some) religion. Whether our life experiences and identities incline us toward our Pressure Parent or our Support Parent persona is within our control.

We cannot change history, revolutionize culture, or choose core aspects of our identity. However, we can decide, with conviction, which parts of ourselves to infuse into our daily parenting and which parts to leave out. Well, mostly. There are those pesky unconscious conflicts that Freud said infiltrate all parent-child relationships. Of course, this part of Freud's theory is non-falsifiable, meaning that we cannot prove it wrong. If we say, "Yes, Freud was correct. I probably treat my child like I do because of some unconscious conflict," then Freud would be right. If we say, "No way. My parenting is not driven by historical relationship factors outside of my awareness," then Freud would say that we are in denial, and he would be right again. (Perhaps we should write a sequel to this book called *I'm Turning into My Parents*. After we sell the movie rights, someone can make it into a B-grade horror movie.) The point is: Whether psychoanalytic theory is valid or not, you can still make intentional, conscious decisions about how you parent.

If you accept these three concepts, then you have successfully pivoted your parenting mindset! The next step is to activate the eight transformations we described in earlier chapters. Once you have read this book in the customary way, we encourage you to pick a different transformation on which to concentrate, each month, for the next eight months. At the start of the month, review the corresponding chapter, and then push yourself to access your Support Parent persona a little more each day. In two-thirds of a year, you will have converted yourself into a more effective parent than you ever thought possible. Best of all, your child's health and functioning will have improved markedly (but not so rapidly that they become suspicious of what you are doing).

GIVING YOUR CHILD AN EDGE

As the culmination to their rejuvenated Support Parent persona, most parents wonder how to help their child perform under pressure. That is an awesome life skill, one that most superheroes consider a prerequisite to their bundle of superpowers. (It is hard to imagine Superman choking just because the fate of the whole world is at stake.) So, here is the recipe, adapted from the corporate CEO playbook I (Hank) cowrote with J. P. Pawliw-Fry. First, the facts.

A person cannot perform better than their best. If the best your child performed on a practice test was 75 out of 100, then they might get 80 on the real thing. But they are not going to get 97 out of 100 unless they cheat. As you now know, most people perform worse under pressure, not better.[4] What *does* happen under high pressure is that people choke, performing considerably worse than their proven best. Thus, giving your child an edge is not about teaching them how to perform some heroic, astronomical, once-in-a-lifetime Hail Mary feat under great pressure. Instead, it is about coaching them how to perform at or just above their historical best, consistently, when it matters most. Performing under pressure is essentially about not choking.

There is a caveat: Parents must accept the fact that their child's best might not be good enough to achieve a particular goal, such as winning a concerto competition, gaining admission to a top school, beating the state record, or having their written work published. Other times, a child's best *would otherwise be* enough to achieve a specific goal, but other factors are at play, such as the number of openings for cello players in the school orchestra, the target percentage of engineering majors in the entering class, the limited funding for a travel team, or the editor's concept for an anthology of maritime fiction.

For example, imagine that your child submits an original short story to a literary magazine. You and her English teacher agree that her narrative is a creative masterpiece, but the magazine rejects it for publication. It would be easy to blame the magazine's editors ("Those idiots!"), doubt the judgment of the English teacher ("She was just telling us what we wanted to hear!"), or change your thinking about your child's talent ("I used to think she was a pretty good writer"), but those appraisals could all be missing the mark. Imagine if what actually happened was that three other fiction submissions that month were just as outstanding, and one of them tackled a theme no one had written about before. The editors had a long discussion and made the difficult choice to reject several high-quality stories with a familiar theme in favor of an equally excellent piece about a novel theme. Everyone tried their personal best. Nobody is to blame. And yet your child did not achieve the desired outcome. Or did they?

It is essential, in circumstances where you know your child tried their best, to praise their effort. (Have we said this enough?) Equally important is to resist the temptation to cast aspersions, unless you have firsthand evidence. It is natural to feel disappointed when your best is not enough to achieve your goal. However, parents can be enormously helpful in these circumstances by saying, "I know you're disappointed. I'm disappointed, too, but not in you. We both feel disappointed that you didn't get what you wanted. Not this time, anyway. Look, we don't know all the factors that went into the decision, but we do know one thing: You did everything you could, and that's something to be proud of. I know you might be sick of hearing me say this, but perseverance pays off. Keep doing your best and you're likely to come out on top one of these times." Both of us have coached clients after disappointing setbacks—from students to CEOs—to play the long game by continually trying their best. And we have repeatedly seen those clients succeed, much to their satisfaction.

An alternative to such Support Parent statements (which you can make sound more natural than we did in writing) is to pay for the desired outcome. Another is to cheat. The parents indicted in Operation Varsity Blues did both for their kids. Legal issues aside, it is impossible to overstate the damage that parental corruption does to kids' self-concepts. Consider this case example:

. . . .

MINDY WAS A BRILLIANT MATH STUDENT AT AN ELITE SEC-
ondary school in the western US. Her grades in other classes were excellent, but math was her forte and, her family hoped, math would be the biggest asset on her application to STEM colleges and universities.

Mindy's father had been an assistant professor in the mathematics department at one of the top schools in the US and now taught at an international school in Europe. With his encouragement, Mindy had joined her school's math team as a ninth grader as was now preparing to compete in the prestigious International Mathematical Olympiad (IMO) in September of her final year. "This is a make-or-break event for you, Mindy," her grandmother had reminded her.

In practice sessions with other members of her school's math team, Mindy had been performing well. Like her teammates, she struggled with the hardest problems. Her confidence waxed and waned, but as the competition drew near, she felt more and more pressure. Her parents, her cocaptain, and even her college counselor had told her that this was her best and final chance to distinguish herself from her peers and construct a strong early-decision application to her first-choice school.

One week before the competition, Mindy was in tears on the phone with her father, lamenting the near impossibility of the hardest IMO problems on the last practice problem set. After a pause, Mindy sobbed, "What can I possibly do to get the right answer on some of these problems that combine number theory, algebra, and geometry? You have to help, Papa, or I'll never get into college."

In one fateful slip of integrity, her father replied, "I was thinking of one thing I can do to help." Mindy sniffled, cleared her throat, and listened while her father described his idea. One of his close friends helped administer the IMO. That friend might be able to screenshot him a copy of the problem set when the competition concluded in his home-country time zone, many hours before Mindy was scheduled to take it.

Then, if her father were able to solve the problems, he could screenshot the solutions to Mindy. And if Mindy were able to memorize the solutions—just to the few hardest problems she did not already know how to figure out—she could get a near-perfect score.

"Papa, what if I get caught?" Mindy asked.

"There's nothing to catch," her father said. "You're just learning more about math before the exam. You've spent so many years studying math already. This is just more math, more learning. Very high level."

Mindy and her father carried out their plan, and Mindy received an outstanding score. So outstanding, in fact, that it caught the attention of another math teacher at school who also happened to be Mindy's adviser. When she insinuated that Mindy might have somehow gotten help on the exam, Mindy became indignant. "What are you saying?" she demanded. "Are you accusing me of . . ."

"The hard thing for me," her adviser explained, "is that you didn't show much of your work for the third problem on day two of the IMO. The math required to solve that problem is far beyond the level I think you're at. I'm asking whether you figured that problem out on your own."

When Mindy told her parents that her adviser had questioned her academic honesty, her father called the principal to complain about due process and repeatedly insisted that no one had any evidence of wrongdoing, only suspicions. "You should be happy that she did so well," Mindy's father insisted. "It reflects positively on the school."

The principal explained that the school had not been in contact with the IMO leadership, nor had the IMO raised any concerns. "However," the principal added, "if Mindy has any improper behavior to tell us about, now would be the time to do it. The discipline committee would look on Mindy's case more favorably if she offered an explanation now than if impropriety were somehow discovered later."

Mindy's father expressed his utter confidence in his daughter's character and mathematical ability. He added how worried he was that false accusations could hurt Mindy's college chances. And by stating to the principal that he was not considering a defamation of character lawsuit at that time, he made it clear that he was.

The next day, Mindy's math team coach asked her to stay after practice, and her adviser joined the two of them for an impromptu meeting. "Could you just go up to the board and show us how you did that last problem?" asked her adviser, handing her a copy of the original test.

"I did it all in my head," said Mindy.

"That's fine," said her adviser. "Just talk us through the steps if you'd rather not write it all out." Mindy tried, but her explanation and notation were paltry. Her coach and adviser waited, hoping that she would admit to somehow getting help on that problem, but Mindy insisted that she had had an insight during the exam.

"It's been so long since the competition that I can't exactly remember what I was thinking," she explained. "And trying to do math in front of two of my math teachers is too nerve-racking. I'm sorry . . . it just is."

Mindy's denial and her parents' unwavering insistence on her innocence and superior intellect left the math team coach, the adviser, and the principal feeling unsettled. But lacking any concrete evidence, the school dropped its inquiry.

Ten years, one bachelor's degree, and one doctorate in neuroscience later, Mindy returned to campus for her class's tenth reunion. Racked with guilt, Mindy found her former adviser and math team coach and made a tearful confession about having cheated on the IMO.

"I've spent the last decade proving to myself that I have decent mathematical reasoning skills. My father refuses to talk with me about the IMO incident, so I think I will carry around our collective guilt for the rest of my life. But the worst part—my lifelong penance—is never knowing what I could have achieved on my own."

· · · · · · · · · · · · · · · ·

Before coaching your child to perform at their personal best under pressure, give them two other well-honed edges: (1) word of honor is sacred and (2) performance on an individual work should be an accurate representation of their ability alone. Of course, you can help your child prepare for tests, competitions, and other performances. Indeed, that is one of the most gratifying parts of our job. But we have to play by the rules. No single, stellar performance is worth years of self-doubt. Our job as parents is to cultivate the opposite: self-confidence.

Now check out **Table 3**, which lays out our best suggestions for helping your child perform under pressure. To the familiar dimensions of importance, opportunity, competition, and perfection, we have added three new dimensions: uncertainty, responsibility/reputation, and incentive. And to double your strategic options, we have created two categories called Pre-Performance Behaviors and Post-Performance Behaviors.

When you compare the **HURTS PERFORMANCE** column to the **HELPS PERFORMANCE** column in **Table 3**, you will notice some familiar themes. For example, parents who frame performances as high-stakes, highly competitive, do-or-die events on which nearly everything hinges are priming their children to choke or quit altogether.[5] You will also notice some new suggestions in **Table 3**, drawn from studies that have asked young people directly about the annoying and helpful things

TABLE 3. HELPING YOUR CHILD PERFORM UNDER PRESSURE

DIMENSION OF PRESSURE	*HURTS* PERFORMANCE UNDER PRESSURE	*HELPS* PERFORMANCE UNDER PRESSURE
	Talking like this to your child will *amplify* harmful pressure and *increase* the likelihood of *choking*:	Talking like this to your child will *diminish* harmful pressure and *decrease* the likelihood of *choking*:
Importance	"This is the most important test of your life." "Your whole future depends on how you play."	"This could be a cool chance to show your stuff." "Remember, it's a concert, just like any other."
Opportunity	"Chances like this come by once in a lifetime." "You've got one shot at this, so kick some butt."	"This tournament is one great way to showcase your talent." "You'll also have another opportunity at the state finals."
Competition	"Everyone at this contest is out for blood." "Look at these other kids; they mean business."	"Feeling keyed up and ready will help you focus." "Pay attention to what you need at this moment."
Perfection	"If this isn't close to flawless, there are always less competitive and prestigious options." "Only a 10 is a 10, baby."	"Your personal best is all that anyone can ask." "It's all about pouring your heart into it."
Uncertainty	"Do you think you studied enough?" "Are you sure you rehearsed your lines enough?"	"You have studied a lot for this final exam." "The more you practice, the more ready you'll feel."
Responsibility & Reputation	"Make us proud, kiddo. I want to post about it." "It's all up to you. Everyone is counting on you."	"We are behind you 100 percent, kiddo. You got this." "You know how to bring the heat. Give it your best."
Incentive	"Just remember how much you love first place." "Don't ever forget why you're doing this."	"Have fun out there" or "Have a great time." [not saying anything about the long-term goal]

CONTINUES

CONTINUED

DIMENSION OF PRESSURE	*HURTS* PERFORMANCE UNDER PRESSURE	*HELPS* PERFORMANCE UNDER PRESSURE
	Talking like this to your child will *amplify* harmful pressure and *increase* the likelihood of *choking*:	Talking like this to your child will *diminish* harmful pressure and *decrease* the likelihood of *choking*:
Pre-Performance Behaviors	Reminding your child about details they already know, such as "Remember to bow."	Providing calm, quiet company as a show of solidarity and confidence in your child.
	Adding new suggestions or task demands, such as "Play the Bach piece as an encore."	Keeping the context and content of the performance as predictable as possible.
	Offering incessant verbal commentary, fidgeting constantly, or stating falsehoods such as "There's no reason to be nervous."	Providing the psychological preparation your child has requested, be it solitude, quiet companionship, or enthusiastic cheering.
	Declaring what your child needs, such as "You need to just breathe right now."	Asking, "What do you need right now?" and respecting whatever answer you get.
	Being verbally directive, such as "Drink more water so you don't get dehydrated."	Silently taking care of what you know your child needs or gently pointing out any essentials.
Post-Performance Behaviors	Offering critical feedback immediately and saying little or nothing about participation.	Praising participation and effort, regardless of the outcome, and waiting to offer criticism.
	Displaying disappointed facial expressions and body language, regardless of the outcome.	Having neutral or positive facial expressions and body language, regardless of the outcome.

their parents say and do before meets, matches, recitals, and other performances. For example, most young people are open to coaching and suggestions during practices and rehearsals. However, most young people experience uncomfortable spikes in pre-performance anxiety when their parents give them directions just before a competition.[6] Telling an elite young tennis player "OK, now is the time when you should warm up and start stretching" will actually hurt performance. Sure, the parent is trying to be helpful, but that young player already knows what to do in the hours before a big match. The parent's remark communicates a lack of confidence. Similarly, parents who are highly critical, extremely negative, or who put talent development above other aspects of a child's life are hurting performance[7] and causing kids to dislike the activity.[8]

Immediately after a game, recital, or show, parents have two other opportunities to help their child perform under pressure *the next time*. First, wait to offer constructive criticism. Kids deserve credit for putting themselves out there. Ambushing them with instant, critical feedback will make them feel more anxious at the next performance. They will be anticipating your postgame routine, and it will increase the likelihood of their choking.[9] Plus, people are physiologically amped up right after a performance. Detailed feedback—whether positive or negative—will be hard to remember.

Second, avoid negative body language, such as facial expressions that say, *I'm disappointed*, or *I'm angry*, or *That's pretty different from what I had hoped for*. Parents have all kinds of thoughts and feelings after a performance, and you should be effusive with the positive ones. The negative ones can wait. Immediately after a disappointing performance, what your child needs more than anything else is affirmation that your love is unconditional. Your presence, your smile, your hug, and every other indicator of love is both comforting and a great way to improve their performance next time.

BE COOL

A lot goes through a person's mind during any important performance—be it a math test, debate championship, or ice hockey game. Different parts of the brain are busy with such tasks as self-monitoring ("How am I doing?"); hypothetical thinking ("Will I remember what comes next?"); emotional expression ("What should this feeling look like?"); social referencing ("How are others responding?"); memory recall ("What was that key fact?"); skill implementation ("How do I do that?"); sensory integration ("Taken together, what do the data from my senses tell me about what is happening in my environment at this moment?"); and both fine- and gross-motor functions (coordinated movements, such as writing, speaking, and hitting a puck). Fortunately, the human brain has about one hundred billion neurons, each with about thirty thousand connections to other neurons. Thanks to the elegant way that consciousness and attention organize all that neural horsepower, we don't hear ourselves ask all those questions. For most people, the experience of taking a test, delivering an argument, or playing a game is manageable, even pleasant. Unless you choke.

To prevent choking and help your child put forth their best effort, use our top tips for *performing under pressure*.

1. **Check your own emotions at the door** so you can be a calm, grounding, pre-performance presence for your child. There is a reason this is Tip 1. As we explained in Chapter 8, strong emotions can be contagious. Wringing your hands and saying, "I think I'm more nervous than you are," is unhelpful. Prevent emotional contagion by coping with your own stress, *away from your child*, such as by confiding in another adult.

2. **Model mindsets that befriend or shrink the moment** by encouraging your child to say, "I welcome this challenge," or "Let's go! Bring it!" A few days before a performance, it helps to shrink the moment by saying things like, "This is just one opportunity among many," or "This is one test/game/interview/match/meet. It won't define me. It won't change who I am inside."

3. **Provide practice feeling pressure** so your child habituates (becomes less sensitive) to the physical, cognitive, and emotional arousal that is normal to feel before and during important performances. The most effective way to help your child habituate to pressure is to practice in settings that resemble the environment in which they will officially

perform. And if possible, get some practice time in the performance space itself. Besides habituating to pressure, your child will also form positive associations with the field, pool, auditorium, rink, ballroom, track, or classroom where the performance will take place.

4. **Create distracting environments** during one or two practice sessions. That way, your child will learn to focus, no matter what is going on around them. In collaboration with your child, have them practice with the television blaring or set a dozen alarms on your phone to go off randomly during rehearsal or practice. If it is safe, have your child practice blindfolded or with one eye and one ear covered.

5. **Teach self-soothing strategies** so your child has several healthy ways of coping with intense pressure. For example: humming a happy tune; slowing breathing to a three-second inhale + three-second hold + three-second exhale + three-second hold (also called "square breathing"); and naming things in the room ("That is a red rug. This is an orange pencil. Over there is a blue vase").

6. **Give them a stress ball** so your child has a discreet but effective outlet for surplus nervousness. Clenching a fist also works well. For most right-handed kids, squeezing their left hand activates the motor cortex on the right side of the brain and helps cut down on obsessive, anxious self-talk—such as "I'm going to bomb this test"—that is happening on the left side of the brain.[10] If this does not seem effective, ask your child to make a fist with their right hand instead. (For some people, language functions, such as self-talk, are localized in the right temporal lobe, not the left.)

7. **Ask them to write down their worries** so their working memory can stay devoted to the task. Writing down worst-case scenarios feels liberating. Some kids also like to read them aloud to a parent or friend. Most kids enjoy tearing, balling, or burning (with adult supervision) their "worry sheet" as a symbolic way of discarding those thoughts. (Journaling about your worries can also help, if done sparingly. Journaling only about worries makes worrying a habit.)

8. **Reduce their self-consciousness** to help your child get used to having an audience. Have them make a selfie movie or set their smartphone to record from a shelf or tripod while they practice. Or have a family member sit and watch them during practices. Temporarily increasing self-consciousness before the real performance will reduce self-consciousness during the real deal.

9. **Show your child how to download a meditation app** so they have a reliable way to achieve mental and physical equanimity. Of all the suggestions on this list, meditation takes the most practice but is the most widely used strategy among elite performers. There are also excellent websites and videos that provide meditation instruction, so you can learn along with your child. And if one or both of you do not have a smartphone, you can access online meditation tutorials from a home computer or the local library.

10. **Adopt a holistic word cue** so your child has a mental anchor. Rather than allowing their thoughts to drift to worst-case scenarios, ask your child to close their eyes and picture themselves performing brilliantly. Then ask them to pick a descriptive word or phrase, such as *confident* or *elegant* or *skilled,* to say to themselves while picturing success. Saying the word later will induce calm and boost confidence.

11. **Create a pre-performance routine** so your child has a familiar script to follow in the hour or two before their performance. Predictability is soothing, and a familiar script allows your child to devote mental energy to the task at hand, rather than to a hundred inconsequential decisions that would otherwise dominate their attention and hijack their good mood. Knowing that your child has an established pre-performance routine also reduces the likelihood of your giving lots of unwelcome directions.

Young people use many other strategies to keep cool under pressure. We invite all parents and children to share their favorite ideas on DrChrisThurber.com/Pressure.

ONWARD

Driven by an instinct to protect, parents push their children toward successful adulthood. In *The Unlikely Art of Parental Pressure*, we have shifted the conversation away from how hard parents push to the way they push. If we parents can get the methods right, then the red herring of intensity swims away. Articles with misguided headlines such as "Are Parents Pushing Kids Too Hard?" may still surface, but the best questions for parents, educators, and youth leaders will be about *how*, not how hard. We have answered the central question, *What are the healthiest ways to push our children?* and left open three other profound questions:

1. What are we pushing our children toward?
2. What are other ways to harness our instinctive drive to protect our children?
3. What is the best advice to give our children for enduring life's many pressures?

Question 1 defines success, so the answer is deeply personal. Parents must answer for themselves, with keen awareness of the forces depicted in **Figure 2**. Question 2 speaks to every aspect of parenting beyond applying healthy pressure, of which there are many. You could spend a lifetime collecting wise answers and still wonder what else you could have done. Self-doubt is an occupational hazard for every parent. And in case you are confident that you *have* done your best, you can trust your child or children to be candid about where you fell short. Question 3 has an actual answer: Play the long game. Rather than being caught up in likes, followers, individual grades, standardized test scores, and comparative prestige, let your core values, a perseverant work ethic, and conscientious care of yourself and others guide you closer and closer to your big goals.

UPWARD

There is tremendous diversity in how parents around the world define success and in how they apply their brand of verbal, nonverbal, and relational pressure. Yet there is uniformity in the goal: to motivate and propel children. Deeply troubling is that our methods can cause great suffering, despite our intention to cause great achievement and gratification. Our objective in this book has been to explain the different paths that lead to these radically divergent endpoints.

In case you have not yet figured it out, you are not a Pressure Parent or a Support Parent. The secret is that we are all both, striving to be Support Parents whenever we can. Now you know how. Of course, future research will yield additional insights about parents' roles in healthy development, but good science and clinical experience have already provided ample practical strategies. We hope we have given you the motivation and methods to become even better at what you do.

AN APPEAL TO PARENTS AND EDUCATORS
How to Dismantle a Fountainhead of Harmful Pressure

• CULTURAL REVOLUTION 1 •

THE FIRST QUESTION I GOT FROM A PARENT AFTER A KEYNOTE address to a large city school district surprised me, but it came as no surprise to the thousands of other parents in the auditorium: "Dr. Thurber, you talked about different teaching styles, but I think our problem is not pedagogy, it's quantity. My wife and I have a smart, hardworking middle-schooler. She plays one sport per term, plays one instrument, and does one club year-round, so we don't think she's overcommitted. But most nights, we send her to bed around 11:30 p.m. and we—her parents—finish her homework. We have to, just so she gets some sleep. What do you think about that?"

I thought about saying the first thing that came into my head, but that is only a good idea on my annual camping trip, deep in the ponderosa pine forests of eastern Washington, with my three best childhood friends.

In a rare display of impulse control (for me, anyway), I stalled to reflect while asking a quick series of informational questions.

> Q: Does your daughter have any kind of learning disability or attention deficit?
>
> A: No.
>
> Q: Is this the experience of other families? (muted laughter throughout the hall)
>
> A: Yes.
>
> Q: Does the school have published homework guidelines?
>
> A: Yes.
>
> Q: And teachers routinely exceed these guidelines in what they assign?
>
> A: Yes.
>
> Q: What do her teachers have to say about this problem?
>
> A: That they are required to cover a certain amount of content, both by the national/state standards and to prepare the students for standardized tests, which, of course, they have to take for college or university admissions.
>
> Q: And what does the school leadership say?
>
> A: They support the teachers. And although they boast about how many students are admitted to top universities, the students' health and happiness seem to be a low priority.

I paused after listening to the answer to my last question, hoping that an intelligent solution would pop into my mind. It did not, so I took my own advice and led with empathy. "What do I think? I think it's incredibly difficult to balance your child's health and her education. I wish you didn't have to make a trade-off because health and education can be complementary." The room was silent, perhaps appreciating my compassion, but clearly waiting for a solution.

I continued, "One nucleus of the problem are the trustees at colleges and universities." That sounded too simple to be true. And the lack of subject-verb agreement conjured an eerie flashback to Mrs. Miller, my chain-smoking, ninth-grade English teacher. I fumbled, "I mean nuclei . . . the root . . . roots . . . ," and recovered: "A board of trustees does the strategic planning. They are the governing body at most colleges and universities. They shape the policies that university presidents or chancellors then direct the deans and faculty to put into practice. That includes directors of studies and deans of admissions. As long as the most important criterion at competitive colleges and universities is exceptional academic talent—as indexed by course grades and standardized test scores—then middle school and high school teachers will continue to feel obligated to cover certain content."

"And elementary school teachers!" one parent yelled from the back. (Muted laughter again peppered the room.)

"The double irony is that most courses at most secondary schools emphasize memorization, and standardized test scores say as much about a family's means as they do about a student's aptitude. Yet when corporate CEOs are asked what qualities they look for in a new hire, their answers are things like: curiosity, creativity, initiative, social responsibility, critical thinking, the ability to collaborate and problem-solve,[1] and—above all—a lifelong love of learning.[2] Until a critical mass of postsecondary schools shift to prioritizing those criteria, your children's teachers will feel tremendous pressure to cover an ever-expanding library of content, and your children will be routinely overwhelmed with the quantity of material they have to master to achieve top grades and test scores."

Now I was on a roll. "The tragedy is that nothing extinguishes a love of learning faster than feeling overwhelmed or, at the other end of the spectrum, bored. Professional educators know that. They see that, just like you. They also know about the science of learning. And they see the bags under your kids' eyes. They know that less able students need more than twice as much time to complete homework than more able students and that the relationship between academic performance and homework time is negative at the individual level.[3] Yet they refuse to enforce homework guidelines or to put limits on the number of extracurricular activities that students can design and in which they can participate. Clearly, sleep and mental health continue to take a back seat to numbers-based college applications. And if content pressure from admissions committees were not the driving force behind the surplus homework that teachers give your kids, then why else would 80 percent of middle and secondary schools continue to ignore the research on adolescents' sleep, learning, and mental health by refusing to start the school day at 9:00 or 9:30 a.m. instead of before 8:30 a.m.?[4]

But what are teachers supposed to do? Most secondary school faculty that I've spoken with in the US, Canada, the UK, Australia, and China have told me the same thing: 'Chris, we know the pace of life at this school is insane, but if we didn't start at 7:30 or 8:00 a.m., we'd never get it all in. And if we limit students' choices, we'll take it in the ear from parents *and* kids.'"

Sometime in the last fifty years, education became more about forcing kids to cram things in than about teaching kids to figure things out.

OUR CHALLENGE

Throughout this book, we have noted many sources of harmful pressure besides parents. From discrimination to constant comparison, they must all be decimated in the interest of our children's health. We chose to focus on higher education in this epilogue because it cuts across race and class and geography, and because it seems more manageable than some other sources of harmful pressure. Until selective institutions of higher education start selecting differently, most of our kids will be overworked and undereducated. The 2020/21 coronavirus pandemic compelled many colleges and universities to revise their admissions criteria. Perhaps an unintended benefit of this health crisis will be its having kick-started creative momentum to solve our pressure pandemic—one that has plagued families for decades.

If decision-makers in higher education held a summit and agreed to shift admissions criteria more heavily toward the human qualities that contribute to a healthy workforce, strong families, and peaceful communities, then our district superintendents and principals could direct their teams of primary and secondary school teachers to overhaul their curricula. Memorization would still be a component of academic mastery, but the emphasis would be on learning how to think, work together, plan, innovate, and make positive contributions to the neighborhood and the world. Extracurricular activities would still be an important part of whole-child education, but the emphasis would be on originality, perseverance, and outreach, not on rank, title, or the length of the list.

Imagine if influential adults rewrote their list of outcomes that mattered. Rather than feeling as if they were drinking from fire hoses, young people would enjoy more *flow* experiences—more encounters with the world that engaged their minds, bodies, or spirits so completely that they would lose track of time.

ACKNOWLEDGMENTS

DR. CHRIS THURBER

I am most grateful for the candor and humility of the parents and young people around the world with whom I have had the privilege of discussing the challenges and rewards of child-rearing. We all share a commitment to betterment—of our jobs as parents and of a world that can be harsh to so many children. I am enormously grateful to my dear friend, the author and publisher Jessica Williams Burns. Her nuanced understanding of narrative, culture, and me were invaluable in shaping early drafts of this book. I am also grateful to Dan Ambrosio and Alison Dalafave, our editor and editorial assistant at Hachette; to Fred Francis and the rest of the Hachette Go production team; and to my own wonderful parents, who have been reading my writing and lovingly offering suggestions since kindergarten. Of course, special thanks to my agent, Alice Martell, for combining the unvarnished truth with ardent advocacy. And finally, I thank Hank for one day stating, "We should write a book together." No pressure, right, Hank?

DR. HENDRIE WEISINGER

First, I thank all of my friends for their support and enthusiasm. Special thanks go to Kenny Cinnamon for teaching me the importance of OLED. Much gratitude to my co-author, Chris, whose talent and thoughtfulness made him the perfect collaborator. Thanks to my agent, Alice, who once again proves she can perform under pressure. More thanks to the Hachette team led by our editor, Dan Ambrosio, who is proof positive that an excellent book has an excellent editor. And finally, like Bond, I am most appreciative of "M," who has energized my life, improved my health, increased my happiness, and framed a lot of loving memories.

NOTES

INTRODUCTION: THE PRESSURE PANDEMIC

1. Whiting, B. B., & Whiting, J. W. M. (1975). *Children of Six Cultures: A Psycho-Cultural Analysis.* Cambridge, MA: Harvard University Press.

2. Yamamoto, Y., & Holloway, S. D. (2010). Parental Expectations and Children's Academic Performance in Sociocultural Context. *Educational Psychology Review*, 22(3), 189–214.

CHAPTER 1: GLORIA AND LIZ

1. Smith, L. (March 12, 2019). College Admissions Bribery Scheme Affidavit. PDF. *Washington Post.*

2. Novotney, A. (2014). Students Under Pressure. *Monitor*, 45(8).

3. American Psychological Association. (2014). Survey Shows Teen Stress Rivals That of Adults. Retrieved November 11, 2019, from apa.org/news/press/releases/2014/02/teen-stress.

4. Lebowitz, S. (2018). 7 Ways Life Is Harder for Millennials Than It Was for Their Parents. BusinessInsider.com. Retrieved July 11, 2020, from https://www.businessinsider.com/millennials-lives-compared-to-gen-x-baby-boomers-did-2018-3.

5. Miller-Day, M. (2003). Parental Pressures a Major Factor for Female College Students Considering Suicide. *Penn State News*. Retrieved November 17, 2019.

6. Wike, R., & Horowitz, J. M. (2008). Parental Pressure on Students. Pew Research Center. Retrieved November 17, 2019, from pewresearch.org/global/2006/08/24/parental-pressure-on-students/.

CHAPTER 2: A LOT IN LIFE

1. Readers interested in the violence sanctioned by certain minorities within minorities may wish to read Jon Krakauer's *Under the Banner of Heaven* or Yasmine Mohammed's *Unveiled*.

2. Zhou, W., & Goh, B. (2020). In Post-Lockdown China, Student Mental Health in Focus Amid Reported Jump in Suicides. Reuters. Retrieved July 12, 2020, from https://www.reuters.com/article/us-health-coronavirus-china-mental-healt/in-post-lockdown-china-student-mental-health-in-focus-amid-reported-jump-in-suicides-idUSKBN23H3J3.

3. Weisinger, H., & Pawliw-Fry, J. P. (2015). *Performing Under Pressure: The Science of Doing Your Best When It Matters Most*. New York: Crown Business.

4. Ibid.

CHAPTER 3: KEEP PUSHING

1. Weisinger, H., & Pawliw-Fry, J. P. (2015). *Performing Under Pressure: The Science of Doing Your Best When It Matters Most*. New York: Crown Business.

2. Rates of mild, moderate, and severe food insecurity vary according to how food insecurity is measured. A 2019 study from the United States Department of Agriculture reported that 12 percent of people in the US experience moderate-to-severe food insecurity. Europe, Central Asia, East Asia, and the Pacific (including Australia) have similar rates, whereas rates elsewhere in the world are higher. Some 55 percent of people in sub-Saharan Africa are food insecure. Smith, M. D., & Meade, B. (2019). Who Are the World's Food Insecure? Identifying the Risk Factors of Food Insecurity Around the World. *Amber Waves: USDA Economic Research Service*, June 3. Retrieved July 7, 2020,

from https://www.ers.usda.gov/amber-waves/2019/june/who-are-the-world-s
-food-insecure-identifying-the-risk-factors-of-food-insecurity-around-the-world
/#:~:text=Using%20the%20FIES%2C%20researchers%20found,percent
%20in%20high%2Dincome%20countries.

3. Capps, L., Sigman, M., Sena, R., Henker, B., & Whalen, C. (1996). Fear, Anxiety and Perceived Control in Children of Agoraphobic Parents. *Child Psychology & Psychiatry & Allied Disciplines*, 37(4), 445–452.

CHAPTER 5: EXPECT *THEIR* BEST, NOT *THE* BEST

1. Rosenthal, R., & Jacobson, L. (1966). Teachers' Expectancies: Determinants of Pupils' IQ Gains. *Psychological Reports*, 19, 115–118.

2. Rosenthal and Jacobson used John Flanagan's 1960 edition of the *Tests of General Ability* (*TOGA*). Flanagan had designed the *TOGA* to measure verbal and nonverbal dimensions of general intelligence, but like other intelligence tests of the time, it had mainstream Western cultural biases baked in, thereby limiting the generalizability (i.e., the external validity) of the Rosenthal and Jacobson (1966) study.

3. Rosenthal, R., & Jacobson, L. (1968). Teacher Expectations for the Disadvantaged. *Scientific American*, 218, 22.

4. Ibid.

5. Gentrup, S., & Rjosk, C. (2018). Pygmalion and the Gender Gap: Do Teacher Expectations Contribute to Differences in Achievement Between Boys and Girls at the Beginning of Schooling? *Educational Research and Evaluation*, 24(3–5), 295–323.

6. Entwisle, D. R., Alexander, K. L., & Olson, L. S. (2005). First Grade and Educational Attainment by Age 22: A New Story. *American Journal of Sociology*, 110, 1458–1502.

7. Fan, X., & Chen, M. (2001). Parental Involvement and Students' Academic Achievement: A Meta-Analysis. *Educational Psychology Review*, 13, 1–22; Jeynes, W. H. (2005). Meta-Analysis of the Relation of Parental Involvement to Urban Elementary School Student Academic Achievement. *Urban Education*, 40(3), 237–269; Jeynes, W. H. (2007). The Relationship Between Parental Involvement and Urban Secondary School Student Academic Achievement: A Meta-Analysis. *Urban Education*, 42(1), 82–110;

Redd, Z., Guzman, L., Lippman, L., Scott, L., & Matthews, G. (2004). Parental Expectations for Children's Educational Attainment: A Review of the Literature. Prepared by Child Trends for the National Center for Education Statistics.

8. Singh, K., Bickley, P., Trivette, P., Keith, T. Z., Keith, P., & Anderson, E. (1995). The Effects of Four Components of Parental Involvement on Eighth-Grade Student Achievement: Structural Analysis of NELS-88 Data. *School Psychology Review*, 24(2), 299–317.

9. Catsambis, S., & Garland, J. E. (1997). Parental Involvement in Students' Education During Middle School and High School. *CRESPAR Report 18*. Baltimore, MD: Johns Hopkins University.

10. Redd, Guzman et al. (2004); Lippman, L., Guzman, L., Keith, J., Kinukawa, A., Schwalb, R., & Tice, P. (2008). Parent Expectations and Planning for College: Statistical Analysis Report. *U.S. Department of Education NCES 2008-079*. Washington, DC: National Center for Education Statistics, Institute of Education Sciences; Lippman, Guzman et al. (2008).

11. Astone, N. M., & McLanahan, S. S. (1991). Family Structure, Parental Practices and High School Completion. *American Sociological Review*, 56(3), 309–320.

12. Eskilson, A., Wiley, M. G., Muehlbauer, G., & Dodder, L. (1986). Parental Pressure, Self-Esteem and Adolescent Reported Deviance: Bending the Twig Too Far. *Adolescence*, 21(83), 501–515.

13. Randall, E. T., Bohnert, A. M., & Travers, L. V. (2015). Understanding Affluent Adolescent Adjustment: The Interplay of Parental Perfectionism, Perceived Parental Pressure, and Organized Activity Involvement. *Journal of Adolescence*, 41, 56–66.

CHAPTER 6: TIGERS, DOLPHINS, AND JELLYFISH

1. Ginott, H. (1969). *Between Parent and Teenager*. New York: Avon.

2. Baumrind, D. (1967). Child Care Practices Anteceding Three Patterns of Preschool Behavior. *Genetic Psychology Monographs*, 75(1), 43–88.

3. Maccoby, E. E., & Martin, J. A. (1983). Socialization in the Context of the Family: Parent-Child Interaction. In Hetherington, E. M. (Ed.), *Mussen Manual of Child Psychology* (Vol. 4, 4th ed., 1–102). New York: Wiley.

4. Sauce, B., & Matzel, L. D. (2018). The Paradox of Intelligence: Heritability and Malleability Coexist in Hidden Gene-Environment Interplay. *Psychological Bulletin*, 144(1), 26–47.

CHAPTER 7: TAME YOUR CORE EXPECTATION

1. Thurber, C. A., & Fair, N. (2019). Crackpot or Cracked Pot? Standardised Testing, Student Mental Health, and the Future of Boarding Schools. *Lights Out*, 12(1), 6–7.

2. Hibbard, D. R., & Walton, G. E. (2014). Exploring the Development of Perfectionism: The Influence of Parenting Style and Gender. *Social Behavior and Personality: An International Journal*, 42(2), 269–278.

3. Termeie, O. (2016). The Impact of Parent Expectations and Home and Neighborhood Influences on Education Goals. Retrieved March 8, 2020, from http://smhp.psych.ucla.edu/pdfdocs/parexp.pdf. See also: http://www.schoolmentalhealth.org/.

CHAPTER 8: INCREASE YOUR WARMTH

1. Black bears are among the notable exceptions. Mothers usually have litters of two to five cubs every couple of years, but when a single cub is born, the mother bear typically abandons it. Biologists believe this is because the threats to the mother's survival, who must lactate and care for her brood for three months without eating, are too substantial to risk on a lone offspring.

2. Psychoanalysts assert that early childhood experiences shape our personality and that various unconscious conflicts (between what we desire and what we can realistically have) are the source of many behavioral and emotional abnormalities. For example, a psychoanalyst might hypothesize that if parents repeatedly and harshly chastised a toddler for peeing their pants, the toddler would grow into an adult who is fastidious

about keeping everything clean. At the extreme, the adult might develop obsessive-compulsive disorder.

3. Behaviorists assert that only external rewards and punishments—not internal, abstract, hard-to-measure thoughts and emotions—explain human behavior. For example, if a parent rewards a child with food or affectionate touch when they cry, then the child will quickly learn to cry when they want to eat or cuddle.

4. Such research methods are unethical and would not be approved or conducted today. Even at the time, many people objected to Harlow's primate studies of extreme isolation. Nevertheless, Harlow's data provided valuable information, just as tragic, real-world cases of severe child neglect have.

5. Bowlby, J. (1958). The Nature of the Child's Tie to His Mother. *International Journal of Psychoanalysis*, 39, 350–373.

6. Ainsworth, M. D. (1964). Patterns of Attachment Behavior Shown by the Infant in Interaction with His Mother. *Merrill-Palmer Quarterly*, 10(1), 51–58.

7. Ainsworth, M. D., & Bell, S. M. (1970). Attachment, Exploration, and Separation: Illustrated by the Behavior of One-Year-Olds in a Strange Situation. *Child Development*, 41(1), 49–67.

8. Rothenberg, W. A., Lansford, J. E., Bornstein, M. H., Chang, L., Deater-Deckard, K., Di Giunta, L., Dodge, K. A., Malone, P. S., Oburu, P., Pastorelli, C., Skinner, A. T., Sorbring, E., Steinberg, L., Tapanya, S., Uribe Tirado, L. M., Yotanyamaneewong, S., Alampay, L. P., Al-Hassan, S. M., & Bacchini, D. (2020). Effects of Parental Warmth and Behavioral Control on Adolescent Externalizing and Internalizing Trajectories Across Cultures. *Journal of Research on Adolescence*. Advance online publication. https://doi.org/10.1111/jora.12566.

9. *Emotional contagion* is an instinctive, primitive form of empathy, a topic we discuss more in Chapters 9 and 10. It is fascinating that human babies, adults, and even dogs all show an emotional response to hearing a human baby cry. See: Yong, M. H., & Ruffman, T. (2014). Emotional Contagion: Dogs and Humans Show a Similar Physiological Response to Human Infant Crying. *Behavioural Processes*, 108, 155–165; and Martin, G. B., & Clark, R. D. (1987). Distress Crying in Neonates: Species and Peer Specificity. *Developmental Psychology*, 18, 3–9.

10. Something called *reactance*, a concept first described by Jack W. Brehm in 1966, might also be happening here. Reactance is unpleasant motivational arousal that emerges when people experience a threat to or loss of their free behaviors. Reactance causes people to think or do things—sometimes impulsively and irrationally—in an attempt to reestablish their freedom. If Nadine felt that her chores threatened her freedom to socialize, then we could see her choosing not to empty the trash as a way to reinstate the time she spends texting her friends.

CHAPTER 9: TURN UP THE HEAT

1. Harris, B. (2004). *When Your Kids Push Your Buttons and What You Can Do About It.* New York: Grand Central Publishing.

2. Lansford, J. E., Godwin, J., Al-Hassan, S. M., Bacchini, D., Bornstein, M. H., Chang, L., Chen, B.-B., Deater-Deckard, K., Di Giunta, L., Dodge, K. A., Malone, P. S., Oburu, P., Pastorelli, C., Skinner, A. T., Sorbring, E., Steinberg, L., Tapanya, S., Alampay, L. P., Uribe Tirado, L. M., & Zelli, A. (2018). Longitudinal Associations Between Parenting and Youth Adjustment in Twelve Cultural Groups: Cultural Normativeness of Parenting as a Moderator. *Developmental Psychology*, 54(2), 362–377.

CHAPTER 11: PRAISE, CRITICIZE, AND QUESTION EFFECTIVELY

1. Seligman, M. E. P. (2004). *Authentic Happiness: Using the New Positive Psychology to Realize Your Potential for Lasting Fulfillment.* New York: Simon & Schuster.

2. Dweck, C. S. (2007). *Mindset: The New Psychology of Success.* New York: Ballantine.

3. Sisk, V. F., Burgoyne, A. P., Sun, J., Butler, J. L., & Macnamara, B. N. (2018). To What Extent and Under Which Circumstances Are Growth Mind-Sets Important to Academic Achievement? Two Meta-Analyses. *Psychological Science*, 29(4): 549–571.

4. Yeager, D. S., Hanselman, P., Walton, G.M., et al. (2019). A National Experiment Reveals Where a Growth Mindset Improves Achievement. *Nature*, 573, 364–369.

5. Lepper, M. R., & Greene, D. (1975). Turning Play into Work: Effects of Adult Surveillance and Extrinsic Rewards on Children's Intrinsic Motivation. *Journal of Personality and Social Psychology*, 31, 479–486.

6. Couples do this all the time, of course. Most spats dispute facts, rather than take a deeper dive into the realm of thoughts and feelings.

7. You can learn more about Dr. Ross Greene's nonprofit organization at LivesInTheBalance.org.

8. American psychologist and relationship researcher John Mordecai Gottman has studied these and other communication dynamics in married couples. He asserts that *how* people argue is more indicative of the health of their relationship than *what* they argue about. One of his major conclusions is: Couples who fight *to understand* their partner during a conflict are far more likely to stay together than couples who fight *to win* the argument. The lesson for parents and children is: Next time you have an argument (which is normal, by the way), stop trying to prove that you are right and the other person is wrong. Instead, try to prove that you really understand what the other person is thinking and feeling. Not only is this technique healthy for the relationship, it may even inspire the other person to do the same for you.

CHAPTER 12: BE THE BELIEVER

1. Marsh, A., Zavilla, S., Acuna, K., & Poczwardowski, A. (2015). Perception of Purpose and Parental Involvement in Competitive Youth Sport. *Health Psychology Report*, 3(1), 13–23.

2. Barger, M. M., Kim, E. M., Kuncel, N. R., & Pomerantz, E. M. (2019). The Relation Between Parents' Involvement in Children's Schooling and Children's Adjustment: A Meta-Analysis. *Psychological Bulletin*, 145(9), 855–890.

3. Khaleque, A. (2015). Perceived Parental Neglect, and Children's Psychological Maladjustment, and Negative Personality Dispositions: A Meta-Analysis of Multi-Cultural Studies. *Journal of Child and Family Studies*, 24(5), 1419–1428.

4. Retrieved July 1, 2020, from https://www.skydiving.com/skydiving/tandem-skydiving/.

5. Vygotsky, L. S. (1978). *Mind in Society: The Development of Higher Psychological Processes.* Cambridge, MA: Harvard University Press.

6. Werner, E. E. (2000). Protective Factors and Individual Resilience. In Shonkoff, J. P., & Meisels, S. J. (Eds.) *Handbook of Early Childhood Intervention.* Cambridge: Cambridge University Press.

CHAPTER 13: OPEN YOUR MIND AND YOUR HEART

1. Curtin, S. C., Heron, M., Miniño, A. M., & Warner, M. (2018). Recent Increases in Injury Mortality Among Children and Adolescents Aged 10–19 Years in the United States: 1999–2016. *National Vital Statistics Reports* 67(4). Hyattsville, MD: National Center for Health Statistics.

2. Also called *sex assigned at birth* or *birth-assigned sex* or *sex recorded at birth,* all of which refer to the construction of a person's sex chromosomes. Retrieved on June 25, 2020, from https://www.who.int/genomics/gender/en/index1.html.

3. The phrases *romantic attraction* and *sexual attraction* are beginning to replace the phrase *sexual orientation,* just as *men who have sex with men* or MSM is replacing the word *gay* and *women who have sex with women* or WSW is replacing the word *lesbian.* These linguistic trends reflect a more nuanced and less categorical view of people's feelings and behaviors. See note 10 below for definitions.

4. CDC. (2016). *Sexual Identity, Sex of Sexual Contacts, and Health-Risk Behaviors Among Students in Grades 9–12: Youth Risk Behavior Surveillance.* Atlanta, GA: U.S. Department of Health and Human Services.

5. James, S. E., Herman, J. L., Rankin, S., Keisling, M., Mottet, L., & Anafi, M. (2016). *The Report of the 2015 U.S. Transgender Survey.* Washington, DC: National Center for Transgender Equality.

6. The term *cisgender* describes persons whose gender identity matches their natal sex. For example, a person whose natal sex is female and whose personal identity is female is cisgender.

7. Deng, C. (2014). China's cutthroat school system leads to teen suicides. *Wall Street Journal,* May 15. Retrieved on July 2, 2020, from https://blogs.wsj.com/chinarealtime/2014/05/15/chinas-cutthroat-school-system-leads-to-teen-suicides/.

8. Marshal, M. P., Dietz, L. J., Friedman, M. S., Stall, R., Smith, H. A., McGinley, J., Thoma, B. C., Murray, P. J., D'Augelli A. R., & Brent, D. A. (2011). Suicidality and depression disparities between sexual minority and heterosexual youth: a meta-analytic review. *Journal of Adolescent Health*, 49(2), 115–123.

9. Mustanski, B. S., Robert Garofalo, R., & Emerson, E. M. (2010). Mental health disorders, psychological distress, and suicidality in a diverse sample of lesbian, gay, bisexual, and transgender youths. *American Journal of Public Health*, 100(2), 2426–2432.

10. Currently accepted definitions of these terms are *gender identity*: how a person, in their head and heart, experiences and defines their gender; *gender expression*: how a person presents gender, through their actions, clothing, demeanor, and so on, and within the context of current social and cultural expectations; *romantic attraction*: being drawn to someone in a tender, amorous, dreamy way that is nonsexual in nature; *sexual attraction*: being drawn to someone in a passionate, physical, sexual way—alone or in combination with other feelings.

11. Valens, A. (2019). Here's what a good LTBTQ ally looks like. *Vox*, June 22. Retrieved on July 8, 2020, from https://www.vox.com/identities /2019/6/22/18700875/lgbtq-good-ally.

12. *Compassion* is empathic understanding of another person's distress combined with a desire to alleviate that distress.

13. Ali Forney Center. (2020). *LGBTQ Youth Crisis*. Retrieved on July 8, 2020, from https://www.aliforneycenter.org/about-us/lgbtq-youth -crisis/.

14. Movement Advancement Project. (2019). *Where we call home: LGBTQ people in rural America*. Retrieved on July 8, 2020, from https:// www.lgbtmap.org/file/lgbt-rural-report.pdf.

15. Harris, D. A. (1999). *Driving while Black: Racial profiling on our nation's highways*. ACLU.org. https://www.aclu.org/report/driving-while-black -racial-profiling-our-nations-highways. Retrieved on July 8, 2020.

16. This active approach to social justice is the essence of being an antiracist. Passively refraining from overt acts of racism, such as not behaving with prejudice, is a necessary but insufficient approach to ending racism. For

an initial in-depth discussion, we recommend Ibram X. Kendi's book *How to Be an Antiracist* and the podcast *Teaching What It Takes*.

17. Noble, A. (2019). Skin Lightening Is Fraught with Risk, but It Still Thrives in the Asian Beauty Market—Here's Why. *Vogue.* Retrieved on July 9, 2020, from https://www.vogue.com/article/skin-lightening-risks-asian-beauty-market.

18. Dadzie, O. E., Petit, A. J. (2009). Skin bleaching: Highlighting the misuse of cutaneous depigmenting agents. *Journal of the European Academy of Dermatology and Venereology*, 23(7), 741–750.

19. Shroff, H., Diedrichs, P. C., & Craddock, N. (2018). Skin color, culture capital, and beauty products: An investigation of the use of skin fairness products in Mumbai, India. *Front Public Health*, 5:1–9.

20. Sidharth Sonthalia, S., Jha, A. K., Lallas, A., Jain, G., & Jakhar, D. (2018). Glutathione for skin lightening: A regnant myth or evidence-based verity? *Dermatology Practical & Conceptual*, 8(1), 15–21.

21. Maritz, D. (2012). *What are the main causes of genocide?* E-International Relations. Retrieved on September 27, 2020, from https://wwwz.e-ir.info/2012/07/12/what-are-the-main-causes-of-genocide/.

22. Weisinger, H., & Pawliw-Fry, J. P. (2015). *Performing Under Pressure: The Science of Doing Your Best When It Matters Most.* New York: Crown Business.

23. Clutton-Brock, T. H., O'Riain, M. J. O., Brotherton, P. N. M., Gaynor, D., Kansky, R., Griffin, A. S., et al. (1999). Selfish sentinels in cooperative mammals. *Science*, 284, 1640–1644.

24. Allchin, D. (2009). The evolution of morality. *Evolution: Education and Outreach*, 2, 590–601.

25. Luthar, S. S., Marc, N. L., & Zillmer, N. (2020). High-achieving schools connote risks for adolescents: Problems documented, processes implicated, and directions for interventions. *American Psychologist*, 75(7), 983–995.

26. Lee, H. (2020). Understanding associations between family economic hardship and primary school-aged children's behavioral and socio-emotional outcomes: Mediating mechanisms and the moderating role of parental social support. *Dissertation Abstracts International: Section B: The Sciences and Engineering*, 82(1-B).

27. Solantaus, T., Leinonen, J., & Punamäki, R.-L. (2004). Children's mental health in times of economic recession: Replication and extension of the family economic stress model in Finland. *Developmental Psychology,* 40(3), 412–429.

28. Oishi, S., Kushlev, K., & Schimmack, U. (2018). Progressive taxation, income inequality, and happiness. *American Psychologist,* 73(2), 157–168.

29. Mohanty, M. S. (2014). What determines happiness? Income or attitude: Evidence from the US longitudinal data. *Journal of Neuroscience, Psychology, and Economics,* 7(2), 80–102.

30. According to journalist Merrill Perlman, "*Intersectionality* was coined in 1989 by Kimberlé Crenshaw, a civil rights activist and legal scholar. In a paper for the *University of Chicago Legal Forum,* Crenshaw wrote that traditional feminist ideas and antiracist policies exclude black women because they face overlapping discrimination unique to them. 'Because the intersectional experience is greater than the sum of racism and sexism, any analysis that does not take intersectionality into account cannot sufficiently address the particular manner in which Black women are subordinated.'" It is worth noting that some scholars have criticized intersectionality theory for its limited applicability. They argue that although one can use intersectionality to describe the multifaceted discrimination that individuals experience, one cannot meaningfully apply it to entire groups of oppressed persons or to systems of oppression, such as slavery.

31. Luthar, S. S., Barkin, S. H., & Crossman, E. J. (2013). "I can, therefore I must": Fragility in the upper-middle classes. *Development and Psychopathology,* 25, 1529–1549.

32. Werner, E. E., & Smith, R. A. (1979). A report from the Kawai longitudinal study. *Journal of the American Academy of Child & Adolescent Psychiatry,* 18(2), 292–306.

33. Luthar, S. S., Kumar, N. L., & Zillmer, N. (2020). High-achieving schools connote risks for adolescents: Problems documented, processes implicated, and directions for interventions. *American Psychologist,* 75(7), 983–995.

34. Luthar, S. S., Curlee, A., Tye, S. J., Engelman, J. C., & Stonnington, C. M. (2017). Fostering resilience among mothers under stress: "Au-

thentic Connections Groups" for medical professionals. *Women's Health Issues*, 27, 382–390.

CHAPTER 14: PUSH WITH PROWESS

1. Zhao, X., Selman, R. L., & Haste, H. (2015). Academic Stress in Chinese Schools and a Proposed Preventive Intervention Program, *Cogent Education*, 2(1). doi: 10.1080/2331186X.2014.1000477; Ping, Y. D. (2018). *Education Blue Book: China Education Development Report*.

2. Boere, J. J., Fellinger, L., Huizinga, D. J. H., Wong, S. F., & Bijleveld, E. (2016). Performance Pressure and Caffeine Both Affect Cognitive Performance, but Likely Through Independent Mechanisms. *Brain and Cognition*, 102, 26–32.

3. Hofmans, J., Debusscher, J., Dóci, E., Spanouli, A., & De Fruyt, F. (2015). The Curvilinear Relationship Between Work Pressure and Momentary Task Performance: The Role of State and Trait Core Self-Evaluations. *Frontiers in Psychology*, 6, article 1680.

4. Weisinger, H., & Pawliw-Fry, J. P. (2015). *Performing Under Pressure: The Science of Doing Your Best When It Matters Most*. New York: Crown Business.

5. Dasinger, T. M. (2014). *Parental Pressure, Anxiety, and Performance Among Age Group Swimmers*. LSU master's thesis. Retrieved July 22, 2020, from https://digitalcommons.lsu.edu/gradschool_theses/4296.

6. Bois, J. E., Lalanne, J., & Delforge, C. (2009). The Influence of Parenting Practices and Parental Presence on Children's and Adolescents' Pre-Competitive Anxiety. *Journal of Sports Sciences*, 27(10), 995–1005.

7. Lauer, L., Gould, D., Roman, N., & Pierce, M. (2010). Parental Behaviors that Affect Junior Tennis Player Development. *Psychology of Sport and Exercise*, 11(6), 487–496.

8. Leff, S. S., & Hoyle, R. H. (1995). Young Athletes' Perceptions of Parental Support and Pressure. *Journal of Youth and Adolescence*, 24(2), 187–203.

9. Scanlan, T. K., & Lewthwaite, R. (1986). Social Psychological Aspects of Competition for Male Youth Sport Participants: IV. Predictors of Enjoyment. *Journal of Sport Psychology*, 8(1), 25–35.

10. Beckmann, J., Gröpel, P., & Ehrlenspiel, F. (2013). Preventing motor skill failure through hemisphere-specific priming: Cases from choking under pressure. *Journal of Experimental Psychology*: General, 142(3), 679–691.

EPILOGUE: AN APPEAL TO PARENTS AND EDUCATORS

1. Partnership for 21st Century Skills. (2014). Resources for Educators. Retrieved on July 1, 2020, from http://www.p21.org/our-work/resources /for-educators.
2. Coleman, J. (2017). Make Learning a Lifelong Habit. *Harvard Business Review*, January 24.
3. Fernández-Alonso, R., Álvarez-Díaz, M., Suárez-Álvarez, J., & Muñiz, J. (2017). Students' achievement and homework assignment strategies. *Frontiers in Psychology*, 8, Article 286.
4. Berger, A. T., Widome, R., & Troxel, W. (2019). Delayed School Start Times and Adolescent Health. In Grandner, M. A. (Ed.) *Sleep and Health*, 447–454. New York: Academic Press.

INDEX